FOR THOSE WHO UNDERSTAND THE POWER AND IMPORTANCE OF THOUGHTFUL DESIGN,

WHICH NOT ONLY RENDERS BETTER FUNCTION, BUT OFFERS A SENSE OF ORDER AND BEAUTY THAT PLEASES, CALMS, AND HEALS.

AND FOR THOSE WHO HAVE HELPED PERPETUATE THIS DISCOVERY:

MY PERSONAL FAMILY: KYLE, EVAN, AND LYNDA,

MY PROFESSIONAL FAMILY: RICHARD RIVEIRE, DAVID DAVIS, AND JEFF RECORDS,

AND ALL WHO HAVE WORKED WITH US PAST AND PRESENT.

INTRODUCTION

The best artists learn to simplify their message, and over time, their work becomes more focused and pure. I am a minimalist at heart and would happily live in a white box with beautiful light. But my influences are varied, and my love of historic architecture, art, and well-edited decoration is deep. I am drawn to both contemporary simplicity and authentic historic ornamentation but to little in between that has been homogenized to pacify those who wish to mildly satisfy everyone rather than lead with a strong point of view. Our Rottet Studio work reflects this dichotomy and the careful use of historic and contemporary design methodology side by side when appropriate. We do not feel that one consistent stylistic approach is correct for all occasions; rather, we see context and purpose as partial directors of the ultimate aesthetic.

Though the style may vary from project to project, we have a series of critical architectural explorations that we have been refining for many years, the results of which are evident in all of our work. These explorations revolve around trying to create interior spaces that are equally dynamic and satisfying as outdoor spaces—or even more so. Interior space does not have the influence of nature, where light, rain, and seasons allow it to take on various visual forms. Interior space is static unless it is designed to be kinetic. I bring spaces alive by creating moments of visual calm, leading to moments of visual intensity, much as a composer creates a musical score that slows and quiets, then strengthens to a crescendo.

Some of our work is pure architectural exploration, and some is more attuned to a specific purpose or individual. I consider the latter work to be set design, as it becomes the architectural setting in which our clients live out their home or work life. It also allows them to present their taste or brand through the built environment. In either case, of exploration or set design, the work has been filtered and edited, and the result represents our point of view through the prism of our passion and process. True art is the expression of an underlying emotion that must be released by the making of that specific work. And thus true art or true design evokes an emotion in those who see or experience it. Being authentic to one's personal roots and sensibility is an important aspect of the design process. No matter what the ultimate stylistic aesthetic is, the result will be unique to the designer and exude his or her underlying passion.

Much as the layers of history make a place a place, the layers of visual experiences form my design. I store visual memories in my mind and access them at the right time to transform them into unique environments. I am sure that many visuals I remember never existed as I have reinterpreted them, and that my memory has blended parts of them together based on what I wanted to experience. Striving to recall, blend, and formulate the perfect composition drives my work. The creation of environments or objects based on imagination and a collection of mental images is the basis of design.

I am pleased when a design is a little unusual or different from what has been seen before, as design is not reproducing what happened in the past but referencing and reinterpreting it to present a unique point of view that could only be of today. In this respect, I recall the words of three designers:

"If you recognize what you are doing, you are not designing, you are copying." —*University of Texas at Austin professor*

"I am happiest when some love my work and some hate it. If this were not the case, my work would not be creation." —*Gae Aulenti, architect of the Musée d'Orsay*

"I was happiest when I was living in Paris just after school. I cleaned out my apartment—empty, to just a bed and the minimal items I needed and loved most." —*Designer Andrée Putman*

Andrée Putman shared that insight with me as I drove her to the Hotel Shangri-La in Santa Monica. With her passion for design, for paring back to what matters most, and her soft-spoken but powerful words, Andrée Putman was an inspiration to me in my work.

My appreciation for well-edited decoration and simplicity began in childhood. One of my grandmothers collected ornately carved and decorative Victorian antiques, and the other simplified her home to almost Shaker-like austerity. I loved both environments and cherished the times when I stayed long enough to soak in the true sense of each. When I got home, I would try out my design skills on the horned toads that lived around our Waco driveway, making houses for them with rocks and sticks and feeling very proud if my home was secure enough to contain them through the night.

My father drove us to almost every museum in the country, and whether he liked the exhibit or not, he would explain that the art expressed the artists' view of what was going on in the world. A particularly memorable exhibition (chickens in cages, in varying stages of molting) was held at the Contemporary Arts Museum Houston, where I now sit on the board. I thought at the time that it could not possibly be art, yet I never forgot the visual of those organic shapes and forms displayed against the minimal white walls. I continue to find art intriguing, frequent the international shows for inspiration, and regularly incorporate art into our work.

Growing up in Houston, watching the skyline of high-rises form, I was so curious about what was inside those magnificent buildings by Philip Johnson; Skidmore, Owings & Merrill (SOM); Pei Cobb Freed. My strict, disciplined father allowed me to take an

afternoon off school one day so I could visit them. Much to my disappointment, I found bland, lifeless interiors inside the lovely structures. Though I put the disappointment behind me and went off to college intending to study medicine, the thought of those wasted opportunities must have stayed with me. While I was taking premed courses, I could not give up art, and I began to attend a number of drawing and painting classes. All I seemed to draw or paint were the spaces within the buildings and what I imagined they could look like. Eventually I realized that I needed to create built environments for a living, and I became an architect and designer.

Right out of architectural school, while working for Fisher-Friedman, a San Francisco architectural firm doing contemporary multifamily housing, I learned how to design inspiring spaces that felt larger by using soaring, tilted, or angled planes; directing views; and keeping materials to an edited minimum. Working with Skidmore, Owings & Merrill first in Chicago, then Houston, I learned to appreciate interior architecture. As designer on a number of high-rise buildings, I loved devising the floor plans, and the adjacent landscape designs, focusing on the details and areas that people viewed most closely. I learned that creating the look of the outside of the building was in many ways easier than creating the inside, as we could make a model of the outside and see exactly how it would appear in the skyline. There is no way to build a model large enough to understand how a space feels as it surrounds its occupants, however. This is where imagination and experience are key. As part of my process, I often stand in an area that has a similar scale to that of the project under way and seemingly stare into space, formulating the design in my mind.

AGNES MARTIN
Cecil Beaton's New York

As high-rise building slowed to a stop in Texas, SOM asked me to move to Los Angeles to head their interiors group. I agreed to a two-year stint and ended up staying in LA for fourteen years. In California, whether visiting museums or out experiencing the contemporary exploratory work of architects such as Frank Gehry and Morphosis and the historic 1920s Mediterranean buildings, I was influenced by all I saw. In particular, California's Light and Space artists inspired me with how they would direct natural light, embed artificial light within a space, or play with light through transparent, translucent, or reflective materials. It was their focused experience of light and sensory phenomena that paralleled my own interests and designs. The work of James Turrell, Robert Irwin, Doug Wheeler, and Larry Bell transformed the way I viewed things. Their techniques still fascinate me and drive my design. I have always placed great importance on the effects of light in terms of reflection, absorption, texture, and shadow, so that visual experiences will never occur twice in exactly the same manner.

Over time, in an effort to create indoor space that is as wonderful as the outdoor environment, I developed and defined my architectural explorations as creating environments that appear larger than their physical boundaries; creating interior environments that are kinetic, not static; creating environments that are uplifting and inspiring; creating environments that continue to surprise and delight beyond the initial impression by offering endless discoveries through the details; and achieving the desired effects by working with light (natural and artificial), reflection, and texture and sculpting planes, volumes, and materials.

Clients, projects, opportunities, venues—all shape the body of work. I have been lucky to live in San Francisco, Chicago, Houston, Los Angeles, and now New York. San Francisco opened my eyes; Chicago brought discipline; Los Angeles brought exploration; Houston brought reinterpretation; and New York, my newest living experience, brings a myriad of influences. Experiencing life in these diverse cities, and enjoying their unique cultures, further supported my determination to design with respect for the influence of the local context—the microclimate of the street upon which a building resides and the building itself. It is important to me to preserve and perpetuate the unique ambiance and culture of a city and neighborhood, as these are what create the joy of travel and discovery.

AUTHENTICITY IN DESIGN

When renovating or designing an interior, there is no reason to re-create design styles of the past if the context is a contemporary building. But if the interior is to exist in an envelope of a certain historic architectural character, it is important to understand that character and choose consciously to reflect or deny it. Any good piece of historic architecture should be taken into consideration, no matter the stylistic quality. For example, the Paris office of the law firm Paul Hastings is set in a building that represents true Boulevard Haussmann design, and it would have been tragic for one entering the grand carved façade to find all of the original detail removed and replaced with unrelated contemporary design.

While I have a great fondness for Modernism, I do not agree with those who feel that design reminiscent of any other style is invalid. Modernism is only one of many architectural languages that have been explored over the years. It is no more valid than Art Deco or Beaux-Arts, which many people in those times felt was the only style. There are some who would say that designing in any style other than what is contemporary or "of today" is invalid. While I actually agree with this statement, because one must design in the influence of the time in which he or she lives, "Contemporary" describes design that is of the moment, a living, evolving entity that cannot yet be classified as any style. And, interestingly, today's Contemporary is really more "New Antiquarian" (a direct nod to the past and ultra avant-garde due to advances in technology). Much as architecture was evolving in the Industrial Age, it is now advancing due to the 3-D printer, which allows complex geometries to be formed. What might have been Modern or Minimal a few years ago

can now be more expressive, with free-form shapes that would have been almost impossible before the 3-D printer.

Designing is not literally copying a style or going back in time (unless you are a museum or theme-park designer). It is, rather, a personal interpretation involving layering in aspects from history onward and choosing to create an environment that evokes emotions, delights, and satisfies. It is, as well, embracing materials and technology of the time looking forward—leaving behind something that advances, even if only in some small way, the art of design, transforming nothing into memorable environments that not only house us but also please, inspire, and motivate us.

Designing a hotel is like being able to dream of anything you want and actually make it happen. Because hotels are not intended as a permanent residence, they are not as restricted and do not have to last a lifetime, though if they are good, they should and do. They can be expressive, unpredictable, playful, and even experimental. In fact, they are theater, with the guest looking to experience something wonderful and unusual. When designing a hotel, I often write a small script, assign it characters, and consider the design from their point of view as if creating a set for a film. I imagine what the characters would need and how they would perceive the space as well as how people watching them would see it. I consider what they see stage right, what appears in front of them and to the left, what the camera sees—as if walking through the film. While designing the Surrey Hotel in New York,

I envisioned it as Coco Chanel's pied-à-terre and began to design it as the set of her high-fashion life on the Upper East Side in the 1920s.

Our more "traditional" designs occur within historic buildings, such as Paul Hastings's office in that classic Boulevard Haussmann building or an Upper West Side residence in a 1908 Italian Renaissance Revival building. In these projects, we preserve the historically significant aspects and create contemporary additions or enhancements that peacefully coexist with the history, or literally reflect it, such as the back-painted glass tables in Paul Hastings's boardroom and in the Upper West Side dining room.

It is sad to see historic buildings with façades that have been amputated and replaced with a "face-of-the-moment" design, looking like a replacement from another species. Don't get me wrong: one can do a careful and valid contemporary addition to a historic building. But one cannot ignore the history and saw it off, as has happened so often between 1950 and now. I would be hard-pressed to design a stylistically traditional interior in a brand-new Contemporary building, but when a building is turn-of-the-twentieth-century or 1920s, as many of our projects' "envelopes" have been, we respect the historic and create a story that reflects this idea: "If time had been good to this building, what would have developed and what would be here today?"

This book explores my work and that of Rottet Studio from 2000 on. As the title suggests, the focus is the principle of designing with authenticity—that is, designing for a purpose that respects and reflects history instead of duplicating or ignoring it. This is design that considers the context based on a strong understanding of history and the present, and design that makes conscious choices to achieve a resultant aesthetic while advancing architectural explorations. The work is part architecture, part set design, part interior design, part graphic design—and all about creating a setting where the inhabitant becomes part of the visual aesthetic and the space becomes experiential art. Though we follow certain conceptual guidelines, we bend the rules and use our intuition for a sense of spontaneity and joy.

MODERN

When clients tell me they want Modern design, I ask them if they truly want Modern or if they want Contemporary with roots in Modernism. Contemporary and Modern are often used interchangeably, yet Modern denotes a certain style from a designated period of time, while Contemporary denotes new styles emerging today. The projects in this section are directly influenced by and rooted in Modernist philosophy. Our project in Frankfurt, for example, is in Gordon Bunshaft's American embassy building—a nice example of pure Modernism. It would have been anachronistic to design the interiors in any other vocabulary, as the goal was to keep the walls as transparent as possible, promote enjoyment of the outside and courtyard views, and celebrate the streamlined functional materials and details of this historic building.

Since early in my career, I have worked with the concepts of the Modern movement, such as simplicity and clarity of forms and elimination of unnecessary detail; materials at 90-degree angles and a visual emphasis on horizontal and vertical lines, notable in International Style Modernism; the notion that "form follows function" so the result of a design and, particularly, its plan should derive from its purpose; visual expression of structure and "truth to materials," meaning that the natural appearance of a material should be seen;

and use of industrially produced materials in a way that celebrates them for what they are. In other words, man-made materials should be used in their invented state and not as faux substitutions for natural materials such as wood or stone.

While there are Rottet Studio projects that I specifically categorize as Modern, the underpinnings of Modernism shape all of our work—even the history-based projects where imagery of a region or a stylistic period is visible. Modernist ideals formed my early education and, later, my art collection from this period. Growing up in Houston, I often visited the Museum of Fine Arts's 1958 Cullinan Hall and the 1974 Brown Pavilion, both designed by Ludwig Mies van der Rohe as additions to the 1924 William Ward Watkin building. The soaring exposed steel columns and large spans holding paintings by Jackson Pollock, Willem de Kooning, Robert Motherwell, and others have forever influenced my design thoughts. This is true not only because the open modern spaces are adorned exclusively with art, but also because of how the minimal Modernist space lives sympathetically with the adjacent historic 1924 Neoclassical building.

Likely the greatest achievement of Modernism and the one that so influences my work was the creation of volumes of interior space and large windows. This meant a space could

visually flow seamlessly from outside to inside, defined by simple forms and true materials rather than dense walls and decorated rooms filled with ornamented furniture. Modernism broke with the pre–Industrial Revolution traditional styles and is related to the age of machination. Building on this history, the advancements in 3-D technology today allow us to create more free-form and dimensionally creative spaces. This has led me to think of space more as a volume that I am carving from within than as an assembly of floors, walls, and ceilings. It would go against the philosophy of Modernism not to take advantage of new technologies or to revert to the restrictive technologies of the Modernist period. Thus, the projects labeled Modern are, in fact, Contemporary with deep roots in Modernism—open, minimal, and truthful, yet sometimes veering from the strict 90 degrees and utilizing more acute angles, curves, or other expressive shapes when they serve a purpose. The Modernist emphasis on diffusing interior/exterior separation is key in our work.

Light plays a major role, whether it is natural from the views or added to lift and expand volumes. Transparency and thoughtful placement of walls and furniture create Modern spatial themes of movement or repose, like visual music.

SEAMLESS INTEGRATION

PAUL HASTINGS LLP, FRANKFURT

FRANKFURT, GERMANY

Our renovation of the interiors of the international law firm Paul Hastings LLP in 2009 offered us the opportunity to work within an iconic Modernist structure in Frankfurt, Germany—the former American embassy, originally completed in 1956 by Skidmore, Owings & Merrill's Gordon Bunshaft. Modernism prevailed in the redesign, true to the building and to our client, who lived in an adjacent Modernist minimal home and whose taste was as modern and minimal as mine. As he noted to me, "This is my day home, and across the park is my night home."

The Frankfurt office is tucked into a tranquil park, and we made every effort to keep the floor plan open to maintain unobstructed views of the park and the interior courtyard. Large bay windows act as clear walls along the perimeter of the courtyard and allow for an abundance of natural light while creating the feeling of an indoor-outdoor environment. Offices and high interior walls were kept clear of the courtyard window wall to preserve the view (a design choice often found in Modernism). The main reception lobby occupies a one-story ground-floor structure with park-like garden spaces and an internal courtyard. By placing a streamlined kitchen behind white paneled doors and through our choice of furnishings, we imparted a residential feeling to the glass-box pavilion.

The space was planned so the conference rooms were located off the main entry corridor. That way, the office retained its openness with sight lines to the courtyard and to our client's night home; the wide corridor serves as a pre-function gathering space as well. Furnishings and materials are minimal and become part of the visual composition of the courtyard, further supporting the client's wish for the overall feeling to be serene yet professional. An ever-changing landscape visually penetrates the interior, providing fresh scenery throughout the year.

PREVIOUS PAGES: A view to the courtyard of the offices for Paul Hastings in Frankfurt reveals the simplicity of the interior design, expressing the clarity of the original 1956 Modernist building by Gordon Bunshaft.

THESE PAGES: Truth to materials was a key principle in the design; the minimal use of color and materials helps seamlessly connect the interior and exterior spaces and reflects a respect for the historically significant building.

TRANSPARENCY

ARTIS CAPITAL MANAGEMENT

SAN FRANCISCO, CALIFORNIA

I was in New York City for an extended period of time, enjoying summer out of the Houston heat, when Stuart Peterson, a technology-focused investment adviser, called me about the design of his San Francisco office. When I arrived at the space and saw the views, I noted that all we had to do was provide sufficient wall space for Stuart's art collection and power for the traders and call it a day—the views from the Bay Bridge to Alcatraz were enough. Stuart founded Artis Capital Management in 2001, and he wanted to create a unique contemporary Modernist space that felt more like a home than a work environment for his employees, in keeping with his company's unique culture.

Due to the nature of the business and the constant visual stimulation of looking at multiple computer monitors all day, our team sought to design a visually quiet space. The office was conceived as a minimal white box. As the white planes peel away, the materials, textures, and colors behind are revealed. Modernist principles of allowing the exterior to flow seamlessly into the interior were incorporated, and no walls touch the perimeter, allowing clear views throughout the space of the entire city and surrounding bays.

Custom handwoven carpet emulates water lapping on the shore. A dark gray cleft stone surrounds the entire floor between columns to reinforce the notion of rippling tides at the water's edge. Along the bay side, incisions were cut into the white box in the ceiling in a pattern that emulates barges in the water visible below. These incisions were then carved away to reveal a warm wood material beyond and provide ambient light. More rigid and orthogonal than the bay side, the city side mimics San Francisco's grid pattern. Six small offices double as mini art galleries. A giant door conceals the work area and, when the door is closed, the room is devoid of visual elements so that the impressive art collection can take precedence. Lounge-style chairs with matching ottomans allow employees to retreat into their "home" and relax. To go alongside the window, we designed rounded chairs that are comfortable but do not disturb the subtle ebb and flow of the tide and sky view.

Additionally, every employee has both a space at the long trading desk in the open office and a private office for personal phone calls. Other amenities include a private conference room overlooking the bay; a teaming room, open pantry, and copy center just off the trading floor; a gymnasium for personal training; a relaxation room; upgraded bathrooms; and a visitor office area, which includes touchdown offices and a private bathroom with a walk-in shower. Traders as talented as these guys are thankful for their luck and skill and therefore a little superstitious—we had to make a home for their first office plant, which they'd had from the beginning. Because traders cannot leave the desk during trading hours, we created a long console, in view of the desk, which is used to display art objects and to set out lunch and breakfast. As trading starts at 6:00 a.m. on the West Coast, the traders really wanted a full kitchen and a griddle to make pancakes, but city codes prohibited it. The residential-style kitchen and console, which conceals not only dining chairs but also exercise balls, serve well to give a family communal table feel.

PREVIOUS PAGES: A painting by Steven Charles at the entrance to Artis Capital Management demands attention and begins the tour of Stuart Peterson's incredible art collection, which is strategically organized to provide even more moments of surprise than those offered by the design of the space itself.

RIGHT: Transparency rules the floor plan, which allows for sight lines from the conference room to the far side of the building. No interior wall obstructs the perimeter window wall with its unparalleled views of the city and Bay Area. Comfortable custom swivel chairs and a carpet designed to emulate water lapping onto the shore animate the window seating areas and offer impromptu meeting spaces.

LEFT: The marble-topped console offers the traders the perfect place to eat lunch and entertain while keeping their desks in sight. Above, ceiling cutouts provide indirect lighting and are intended to mimic barges docked in the bay. Artworks on the wall include pieces by Doug Kerr (left) and Dave Muller (right).

ABOVE: Workout balls are tucked into the console end, which is lined with lively paper designed by Hanna Werning and illuminated by fluorescent lights to enforce the visual surprise and color.

Risky Business
JANE BIRKIN & SERGE GAINSBOURG
JE T'AIME
ROEDELIUS – LUSTWANDEL – GYR 6628-2
THE ZODIAC . . . COSMIC SOUNDS
4 TRACK
7½ IPS
STEREO

OPPOSITE: When tucked away, dining chairs appear of a piece with the warm, limed oak burl wood of the console table, but they can also be removed for additional seating.

ABOVE: Storage cabinets lined with festive patterns by Hanna Werning hide behind the sliding panels.

ABOVE: A table of my design was built for function and convenience and serves as a practical-yet-artful storage device. The sliding surface panels reveal storage compartments with colorful details by Hanna Werning.

RIGHT: A large painting by Matthew Ritchie hangs over the seating area at one end of the trading floor. Chairs by Fabien Baron surround the low table.

MAGNUM
MAGNUM

VISUAL MOVEMENT

AGNES MARTIN
BESPOKE HOME

ROTTET RESIDENCE

MONTAUK, NEW YORK

Without any intention of buying a property in the Hamptons and after having looked for ten years on the West Coast for my second home, I was captivated by this Modern house designed by George Nelson and bought it the day I saw it. While visiting the East Hampton residence of my New York partner, David Davis, I was perusing the local real estate magazines, as I love to look at houses. When I saw that there was a George Nelson–designed home for sale, I immediately called the realtor, pretended to be interested in buying, and asked her to show it to me. She noted that Montauk is very far away and I replied, "What's twenty minutes when you're coming all the way from Houston?" The home and Montauk have stolen my heart.

I see why artists and writers love putting down roots in eastern Long Island—the quality of light, the stars, the quiet, nature, and the sea are addicting and inspiring. I often work from the home, which is composed of a series of hexagons that, in Modernist fashion, allow the spaces to flow among different abstract compositions of volumes and planes. And the breezes and creative energy flow endlessly. Without 90-degree corners, there is a feeling of continual movement that is amazingly inspiring for creativity but not so conducive to focus. I joke that I need to build a little rectangular chamber to allow me to concentrate on the details of a design once I have created it.

The Midcentury Modern Shingle-style house was originally designed by Nelson and Gordon Chadwick and built in 1961 on the shores of Montauk for O.R. (Dick) Johnson's parents. It employed many of the Modernists' principles of letting in as much natural light as possible, framing the views, and using an open plan and even what Le Corbusier called the idea of Promenade Architecture, which included a ramp as well as a stair. Dick Johnson was instrumental in preserving Montauk's forest land, and he held many meetings of the preservationists in the beloved home. Circumstances forced him to sell it, which he did with the stipulation that it would never be torn down. The buyers did not comply. When Dick heard that it was being demolished, he asked to be given the original built-in cabinets, furniture, and anything else that could be salvaged. He later rebuilt the home to its exact state (with a few strategic modifications to relate to the new site's differing views) using the original cabinetry and designs from the 1961 house.

At first I wanted to pull out the quirky kitchen cabinets and change the odd yellow and gold colors, but I was slow to renovate, as I thought I should live with Nelson's design for a while. I came to respect the genius of it and began to restore and add like a collector rather than alter the original design. I kept the existing kitchen but converted the overly large utility room into a bedroom and bathroom, taking advantage of every odd corner available within the hexagonal space; refinished and added hardwoods throughout; restored the interior shingles; found paints to match the original gray colors as closely as possible; and added a pool surrounded by the flagstone Nelson had used in the lower-floor living area, allowing it to flow from inside out in true Modernist style. In landscaping, I was careful to plant only species indigenous to Montauk and only around the pool and immediate borders of the house to preserve the "home set in the wild" feeling appropriate for its location. A few vintage Modern pieces from the original house came with it, such as the Nelson Marshmallow sofa, a Paul McCobb credenza, and some vintage McGuire rattan. Over time, I have collected vintage Modern furniture

PREVIOUS PAGES: Geometric shapes, specifically hexagons, dominate my Montauk home, which was originally designed by George Nelson. I designed the interiors to emphasize the property's unique planes and volumes; these are especially visible in the living room, which includes some of my own furniture designs and a self-portrait by Kiki Smith.

OPPOSITE: Circular skylights illuminate the upstairs corridor, which features original George Nelson built-in cabinets with sliding doors.

pieces by Nelson and other designers such as Raymond Loewy, Arne Jacobsen, and Franco Albini, which dwell next to my own furniture prototypes.

The art seems to come to the house like bohemian artists flocking to the East End. I had bought a large Kiki Smith last-minute at an art show and did not hang it for five years as I did not have ceilings high enough. When I purchased the Montauk home, I had the work framed and hung. When I saw it after five years, I called the gallery owner and told him he had shipped the wrong piece, as surely I would not have bought a self-portrait of Kiki Smith reaching for a self-portrait of her head. Now I often watch people dancing around the large octagonal living room with their hands up oddly like hers and wonder what kind of mysterious coincidence this particular piece of art is. A large Larry Poons drip painting hangs over the stair—he was already famous when I was an art major before switching to architecture. Other than an Alexander Calder, the rest of the artworks are by young, lesser-known artists mostly from Chicago, Houston, and New York City. The pieces keep me company in the winter months when no one wants to join me in Montauk. Accessories range from artists' books, such as Tauba Auerbach's incredible pop-up book, to midcentury ashtrays and pottery purchased in Palm Springs. Outside, I am happy to have Patricia Urquiola's nicely designed lounge chairs and rug.

Preserving the well-thought-out details, materials, and colors of Nelson's original design proved to be the right choice. I can create a sleek, minimal environment anywhere at any time in the future, but I never could have re-created the authentic and remarkable feeling this house has. It is truly one of a kind and a testament to the principles of Modernism.

PREVIOUS PAGES, LEFT: An Alexander Calder rope weaving draws the eye above a vintage bronze inlay bench at the stair landing.

PREVIOUS PAGES, RIGHT: A Larry Poons drip painting hangs underneath a vintage Louis Poulsen light.

OPPOSITE: I specifically designed the Floating Table, a signature piece from the Rottet Collection furniture line, for this hexagonal dining area to reflect the natural elements from outside and appear as if it is levitating within the space.

ABOVE: A detail of the dining area reveals the original built-in wall clock and geometric screen separating the dining room from the hallway. A Paul McCobb credenza is adorned with vintage accessories from my personal collection.

OPPOSITE: In the master bedroom upstairs, a 36-inch-diameter vintage skylight sits asymmetrically over the bed, which Rottet Studio originally designed for the James Royal Palm Hotel in Miami. Due to the subtle side mirrors, drawers, and convenient access to power, it became a personal favorite. Vintage lights and a painting by Andrew Brischler complete the space.

ABOVE: On the other side of the room, yellow ochre-colored doors frame a vintage George Nelson bookcase and a painting by Andrew Holmquist. The master vanity is a vintage, solid-surface, freestanding hexagonal-shaped form.

The back of the home becomes the front due to the car culture and true to the Modernist approach called Promenade Architecture, popularized by Le Corbusier. A ramp leads from the driveway to the upstairs kitchen. George Nelson and Gordon Chadwick reinterpreted the Hamptons' predictable stone and shingle style in a Modern aesthetic. I simply restored and preserved the engaging façade.

COMMON WEALTH
François Truffaut
OnCukor
TALKING PICTURES PHOTOGRAPHS BY ELLEN GRAHAM

REFINED ORDER

FINANCIAL MANAGEMENT FIRM

NEW YORK, NEW YORK

When Rottet Studio designed the midtown Manhattan offices of an international asset management firm, the client—who had seen numerous published projects of ours—trusted us to transform their current office style. Due to the Manhattan skyline views, the low ceilings, and the client's fastidious nature, we chose to design the space using the Modernist principles of bringing the outdoors in by focusing the views, embracing the intimate nature of the low ceilings where necessary, and incorporating strong order into the plan.

We created a two-story reception space with an open staircase set against, and anchored by, a backlit onyx wall that imparts a warm glow and complements the fabulous views of the New York skyline. The open staircase between floors provides a grand space and lovely backdrop to the reception area and helps maintain communication between floors. Clear glass office fronts along the exterior wall and light-colored stone flooring bring natural daylight into the space from the perimeter. Due to the sound reduction and discretion required by the client, we achieved the maximum level of acoustic privacy while maintaining the access to daylight by building a special system of walls made of two panes of glass sealed to provide an air space that buffers the transmission of sound from one space to another.

In order to provide visual interest and a contrast from the subdued Modernist walls, we curated a collection of select art photography. Instead of just hanging the art on the walls as in a gallery, we sought out or commissioned specific works that filled entire walls, such as the large-scale work by Miles Coolidge featured in the boardroom's anteroom and the oversized commissioned works from Robert Longo and Camille Seaman. A Reinhard Görner photograph of a hallway was placed at the end of the hallway leading to the conference center, creating a visual illusion that the corridor goes on forever into the fanciful world of the photograph.

TIME
The Illustrated
History of the World's Most
Influential Magazine
Norberto Angeletti / Alberto Oliva

PREVIOUS PAGES: A collection of fine art photography dresses a financial management firm in New York. Above the reception lounge hangs a large commissioned wave by Robert Longo, while a Reinhard Görner photograph of a museum corridor lends the illusion of infinite space to an otherwise short hallway.

LEFT: A photograph by Miles Coolidge adds texture to a waiting area with a low round table by Minotti and chairs by Monica Förster for Bernhardt.

ABOVE: The organic shapes of a custom carpet contrast with the angled chrome features of a chair by Minotti.

RIGHT: A relaxed waiting area with a custom rug provides a residential atmosphere for the office. The floor-lit pier support, white onyx wall, and light-colored marble floor add luminous clarity to the design. The artwork by Camille Seaman was commissioned for the client's collection of contemporary art photography.

FULL MOON

ABOVE: The management company's conference room offers an abstract unlimited view of the Manhattan skyline in two directions. A lengthy custom-designed burl wood-topped table and built-in seating lining one wall emphasize the large volume of the space.

OPPOSITE: A minimal lacquer and limestone stair floats in front of the perimeter glass wall. The step and its trim were left exposed to visually lighten the stair and integrate it into the skyline view beyond.

REFLECTIVITY & ILLUSION

PAUL HASTINGS LLP

NEW YORK, NEW YORK

There are points in a design career when one meets a client who becomes a friend and a patron for life. In 2002, our Los Angeles client and friend Pat Ramsey sent me to New York to meet with the managing partner of the law firm Paul Hastings so I could hear firsthand that they wanted open, clean, minimal Modern offices not only for their new Manhattan space but also for all of the offices that they would be opening around the world. Seth Zachary, the managing partner, explained to me that they sought to defy the aesthetics of the old dark law firm and create an inspiring, light-filled, livable work environment for the attorneys and staff who spent so many hours in the space. They and I knew then what others are now beginning to realize—if you design an office to be more like a beautiful home, the office serves better to relax, motivate, engage, and inspire loyalty from the staff. To that end, the reception area acts as a living room, there is a wonderful kitchen-like space with a view, furnishings feel residential and comfortable, and people are allowed to work in and enjoy the entire space, not just their small office component.

For Paul Hastings's New York office, we consolidated the firm's two prior New York locations onto eleven consecutive floors in a Helmut Jahn–designed high-rise in midtown. They were relocating from a building with unobstructed views into one with less-than-ideal views. My clients challenged me to be so creative that the attorneys would love this space far better than they did the one right on Park Avenue with stunning views.

The floor plan of the new building was unusual, with its noncentral core, irregular angled corners, nonuniform column spacing, and natural light on only the two ends of the building. Consequently, we chose to arrange the floor plan with support spaces—a conference room, files, and a pantry—in the center and private offices lining the perimeter; we avoided the two ends so as to allow natural light into all areas of the space.

At the end of the corridor off the elevator lobby we placed a glass staircase linking the conference center with all eight typical attorney floors above. Located where all could experience the visual, the staircase served as a connector for the floors and as a bit of theater—throwing in natural light from outside, reflections off the back-painted glass and polished stainless walls, and the movement of people running up and down. My favorite moment of the project was when one of the partners (who had very traditional taste and wanted all dark wood everything) stopped me in the corridor and said, "You're the design lady, right? I just wanted to tell you that I love the office space, and all of my clients do, too. It's like living in a modern tree house with all the conveniences—it is so much fun." I was instantly forgiven for not resorting to the use of traditional ornamentation that was still common in law office design then.

To further enhance the theme of "endless space," we created a series of forced-perspective corridors, dropped angled drywall soffits, and tapered walls. To reflect and emit light throughout the project, we used glass for doors, walls, and counter surfaces. This technique, along with the similar white angled walls and undetectable mirrors, was used to help visually extend the space. Likewise, this design adopted custom administrative workstations with articulated angles and tapered sides. Thanks to the challenge of this project, I began my career-long design exploration into how, with the correct use of light, materials, and forms, you can create an environment that feels far larger, more expansive, and more dynamic than its physical boundaries.

PREVIOUS PAGES: A commissioned art piece by Linda Hudson featuring tall columns made of capillary beads graces the entrance to Paul Hastings's New York City office. A backlit white onyx wall extends to the ceiling of the double-height reception space and creates a dramatic first impression.

OPPOSITE: A high-gloss resin wall reflects the movement of the stainless steel and dichroic glass elevator wall.

ABOVE: In the conference center, a lacquer and marble concierge desk sits in front of a burl wood and textured glass wall. A Roy Lichtenstein screen print on stainless steel hangs to the right.

OPPOSITE: In the elevator lobby, natural stone flooring was used in association with brushed stainless steel to represent the human ingenuity of creating buildings from the earth as well as the history of vertical elevation in the city that never sleeps. The detail of the inset call-button made of dichroic glass symbolizes the growth of technology.

MODERN:
EXPLORATIONS IN VISUAL MOVEMENT

In recent Modernist projects, I have been consumed with the idea of "focusing the eye." The intention is to create a sense of motion that animates the space. In the lobby concept shown here (right and opposite, above), strong vertical lines draw the eye up and over the ceiling and back down to the fireplace hearth. By contrast, the definitive horizontal planes of the hearth draw the eye to the back wall made of reflective glass and bronze, which shimmers and changes as one draws closer, giving the appearance of movement. In a penthouse in Houston (opposite, below), framing the views and allowing nature to penetrate inside seamlessly promote the illusion that the space expands beyond its physical boundaries.

MINIMAL

I characterize a certain number of our Rottet Studio projects as Minimal because they express the essence of the design through eliminating all nonessential forms, features, or elements. Minimalism results when the simplest, fewest elements are used to create the maximum effect. Following art as I have for many years, I find that many of the best artists' work becomes more minimal and reduced to the most effective visual statement as the artists mature.

In art and design, Minimalism is not merely a final development of Modernism but also a shift toward expressing the design intent in the most reductive manner. Minimalist design does not require texture, color, or fine materials. It is created through the use of light, focusing the eye of the occupant, and through the manipulation of forms and volumes. Often it is composed of only one or two colors or materials, such as white drywall and wood floors.

Since collecting art has been one of my life passions, Minimalism in design offers me the best way to create a unique setting where there is a respectful interplay between the concepts of the artworks and the concepts of the physical setting. I love the creative process of this collaboration and juxtaposition.

As a specific design movement, Minimalism is identified with post–World War II

Western art and particularly with American visual arts in the 1960s and early 1970s, when artists Donald Judd, John McCracken, Agnes Martin, Dan Flavin, Robert Morris, Ronald Bladen, and Anne Truitt dominated the scene. Minimalism has earlier roots in the geometric abstraction found in the art of Kazimir Malevich, Piet Mondrian, and artists and designers of the Bauhaus and its later followers, still supporting Ludwig Mies van der Rohe's often-repeated dictum that "less is more." Minimalist interior design is central to the twenty-first century. It is surprisingly inviting in its spare and streamlined forms and neutral colors. Less clutter frees the mind, and the beauty of each piece of furniture or art in the space can easily stand out.

Early in my career I felt the power of Minimalist architecture when I experienced the installation artworks of James Turrell and other California-based Light and Space artists. It was a profound experience to see Turrell's skyspace installations, a passage to a small viewing room with an aperture in the roof to glimpse the sky. In these, Turrell makes the sky "within reach." In all his works, his manipulation of light defines space, or the illusion of it, to create an indeterminate portal that feels timeless and infinite. Several years into my exploration of Minimal interiors, I visited Dia:Beacon, a converted factory along the Hudson River that houses large works of installation art. There, I was influenced by artists such as Fred Sandback, who created powerful rooms with nothing more than a red string nailed taut to the ceilings, floors, and walls. Stepping across the thin string brought a sense of exhilaration, as if I was transforming as I moved from one monumental setting to another. In my purest Minimal projects, I attempt to accomplish a similar feeling.

Our designs draw upon the elements of Minimalism, including open, organized space planning; a single neutral base color—often white; bare floors of concrete, stone, or wood; limited accents for focus or color; unobstructed walls hung with one or two pieces of art; a few pieces of necessary, well-designed, and strategically placed furniture and tabletop pieces; and unseen lighting sources. We utilize sleek built-in storage for useful, practical items so no clutter is visible. Minimalism is essentially the art of aesthetically living with less. A beautiful, functional office or home with a Minimalist theme is one of the hardest to design because it requires discipline, skill, precise details, and the right client. I always try to create a sense of *presence*—as I experienced with the Sandback room—and use a few choice materials to provide tranquility and pure simplicity.

CAPTIVATING QUIET

BERNHARDT DESIGN SHOWROOM

NEW YORK , NEW YORK

Bernhardt is one of the most significant furniture manufacturers in the United States, and certainly one of the most well respected for design innovation. When Bernhardt's president and creative director, Jerry Helling, asked me if I wanted to help him with the New York City showroom, I was flattered. I have worked with him and marketing director Carolyn Smith in the design of their showrooms for almost twenty years and have watched the brand mature and excel.

As any well-informed design patron would, Jerry came to me knowing what he wanted for the plan layout and how he felt it should function in order to show the company's greatly expanded line of products. Conceptually, we wanted to continue in the spirit and attitude of the Chicago showroom we had previously designed, which had a white, ethereal residential loft feel with very few walls—just enough to display the product properly. In New York, our challenge was to create an intimate, comfortable feeling within a space twice the size of the Chicago showroom. True to Jerry's magic touch, he decided on a midtown location that is now becoming a mini contemporary design district for New York City. With our affinity toward opening views to passersby, we placed the main chair display and walkway along the windows and devoted the internal section to the display of the case goods and tables. We lined the perimeter with sheer drapery to give a gentle sway of motion to the space.

The reception desk and backdrop wall clad in white Calacatta marble hover above a white terrazzo floor. The side wall is canted back to lead the eye to the receptionist, and other walls are "held up from the floor" as planes that seem to float in front of the structural wall and visually extend the welcoming reception area into the display. A backlit Krion panel shields the side view and conceptually ends the pattern created along the window wall. Columns and white vertical light planes provide backdrops for the displays. The space is devoid of color, and the fabric and carpet were chosen to hint at the idea of wool or cotton in their natural state before being color treated. The Minimal finishes and materials used in the architecture and furniture played a significant part in the overall design; they are all visually quiet so as not to interfere with the lines and detailing of the furniture.

PREVIOUS PAGES: Throughout the Bernhardt showroom in New York, Rottet Studio used minimal, neutral materials to accentuate the furniture pieces. The hardwood barstool seats and streamlined sculpture contrast with the white bar area, and a brilliant red sofa adds color to the reception area. A Calacatta marble wall stands behind the marble reception desk, while the left wall was canted backward to subtly direct attention to the receptionist.

THESE PAGES: White walls, ceiling planes, and Calacatta marble elements reflect off a white terrazzo floor to create the illusion of clouds floating in the space.

ABOVE: A fabric sample wall offers a colorful and interactive area in which to explore endless options and possibilities.

OPPOSITE: At the showroom entrance, visitors are greeted with a dynamic design where planes do not quite connect, which allows a brief glimpse of the products that await.

Seemingly heavy walls lit from below appear to float and stop before reaching the ceiling in a manner that diffuses their structural reality and directs attention to the products instead.

RAW BEAUTY

GOCHMAN RESIDENCE

HOUSTON, TEXAS

We had just the right kind of open-minded client in Molly Gochman, a private artist-collector who wanted a Minimal space to serve as her home, office, and art gallery. Commissioned to redesign her 1980s condominium—which she had chosen for its proximity to the best fitness and yoga studios in Houston, the park-like setting of the grounds, and the skyline views—we combined two penthouse units into one large residence on the entire twelfth floor at the historic Houstonian Estates.

This Minimal design focused on both raw and refined elements. The concrete elevator core wall and structural columns were discovered during demolition and revealed a constant yellow line from the original construction of the building, which was used as a point of reference and a subtle accent to the design. The gray concrete core walls complement the thick white marble stone tops and stainless steel fixtures and help provide a juxtaposition between the elemental and the polished. The home utilizes only five materials: natural rift-cut oak flooring, natural concrete, white-painted drywall, white Calacatta marble, and stainless steel. Pratt & Lambert's Silver Lining white paint was used throughout.

In an effort to exploit the uncompromised views from this twelfth-story perch, we incorporated floor-to-ceiling windows with automatic shades in every perimeter room. Four balconies, one at each corner of the unit, further connect the resident with views over all of Houston, including downtown, the medical center, and the Galleria. The barely furnished space has an open floor plan spanning 5,000 square feet. One half of the combined space was designed to serve as an office and art gallery with a separate kitchen for catering events, while the other half was designed for comfortable, minimal but luxurious living with all the amenities one could imagine, including another private gourmet kitchen and a soaking tub imported from Italy.

PREVIOUS PAGES: Demolition during the creation of the Gochman residence revealed construction lines on the raw concrete of an original elevator core wall; they provide a sense of industrial archeology—both ancient and radically new in spirit.

LEFT: The industrial feel of the concrete wall and its inherent imperfections contrast with the meticulous craftsmanship and sophistication of the kitchen.

ABOVE: Views of the Houston skyline at dusk flank the mirror in the master bathroom. The cantilevered marble counter with large central trough appears to levitate due to the use of clever lighting tricks.

OPPOSITE: Simplicity and clean lines are prevalent in the guest bathroom, and marble elements are structured to appear natural, as though they were sliced directly from the quarry.

TRANQUIL ILLUMINATION

BERNHARDT DESIGN SHOWROOM

CHICAGO, ILLINOIS

When the Bernhardt Design showroom moved locations within the Chicago Merchandise Mart to the opposite side of the building, the move created a challenge. The new space decreased Bernhardt's square footage significantly and replaced their coveted views of the Chicago River with views of the underside of the L train. When we designed the first Chicago showroom, we had decided to do what no other showroom in the Mart did. All of the others followed the Retail 101 rule to "focus the view on the product for sale and do not distract the buyer." We chose instead to open the showroom to the exterior view and treat it like a Chicago loft home that welcomed in designers and clients as if they were friends who were welcome to stay all day if they liked.

True to the kind and gracious personalities of Anne and Alex Bernhardt, the founders, this approach also proved to be what Jerry Helling, Bernhardt's president and creative director, and Carolyn Smith, their marketing director, wanted. The original Bernhardt Chicago showroom had light-colored wood walls designed on spring-loaded clips so they could be easily moved to change the room's scenes and displays. In keeping with the Minimalist approach we were adopting, we chose to eliminate extraneous materials such as wood from the new showroom but to keep the open, residential loft-like attitude, which we re-created through a number of explorations with light, angles, and materials. For this showroom and the future ones, we as a team decided not to commit to a wood color but instead to utilize white as a backdrop, with the aim of emulating a Minimal museum setting. This would allow us to display the furniture as art and for visiting designers to create their own palettes for their projects with Bernhardt's wood, metals, leathers, and fabrics.

The plan was designed to visually enlarge the feeling of the space while creating small vignette showrooms so that many different scenes can be displayed at once. We detailed the walls with a knife edge to help create movement around the space, so the walls appear light and ephemeral and there is never a visual end to them; the walls never touch each other. Instead, they continuously create a view into another space to help entice visitors to be adventurous and explore what they can see in the next room. The ceiling over the furniture display areas appears to float; painting it black contributed to the illusion that it never ends. Our design team utilized light as the medium for solving the spatial challenge as well as the source for extending the perception of space. Light-paneled walls were also used as reflective accents to create the appearance that natural light leads one into the space beyond.

In the world we created inside the showroom, we focused the viewer's attention on the art, which is, in this case, the furniture. An ephemeral wall serves as the backdrop for Bernhardt's chair display. The wall is composed of metal painted white with a custom-designed perforated pattern. A fabric scrim was stretched behind the panels to disperse the light, creating a consistent glow. The floor that aligns with the paneled wall is made of shiny white epoxy resin to help reinforce the idea of a plinth, but it was set flush, allowing the product to be accessible and inviting for anyone to sit on and touch and thus become part of the scene and experience.

PAGE 106: Light, angles, and materials brought a new Minimal museum spirit to Bernhardt's Chicago showroom. Vignette display areas are framed by walls that, seen on an angle, offer views into another space and evoke a sense of curiosity.

PREVIOUS PAGES & RIGHT: Allowing light in but blocking views to the L train, perforated sheet-metal panels are backlit to create a sense of whimsy and encourage visitors to explore the showroom.

LEFT AND ABOVE: A white lacquer box encloses the recessed marble-faced bar. The downlit feature wall behind the bar was introduced to highlight the horizontally striated stone, which repeats in the recessed stone panel of the counter.

NEXT PAGES: A view from behind the bar offers a serene look at the use of light and materials, and their reflections.

MINIMAL:
EXPLORATIONS IN CONTEXT

When the environmental surroundings are naturally beautiful and the goal is to be one with them, a Minimal design is key. The floor and ceiling materials in a resort room (right) embrace and reflect the surroundings, flowing from inside out to make the suite one with the shore. In the concept design for a residential tower in Yokohama (opposite, above and below), I used expressive form and reflection to embrace the sea. The residential tower was envisioned as being protected like a pearl within an oyster shell. Bronze glass mirrors the sea and encompasses a curved opalescent white lining that contains the homes.

BEAUX-ARTS

When designing an interior environment, we first consider the context. Though it is possible to create an interior that has no relation to the building in which it is housed, doing so should be a conscious decision, as an interior typically feels more rooted, logical, and pleasing if it is an extension of the exterior in some way.

We have had the good fortune to work within several historic Beaux-Arts buildings in Manhattan and Haussmann-influenced buildings in Paris, and within my own early 1920s Southern Colonial/Neoclassical home in Houston. As well, for certain hotels, we have been asked to create an ambiance of traditional charm rooted in Beaux-Arts luxury and style. I categorize projects as Beaux-Arts style when the ultimate aesthetic is influenced by an existing historic structure or a sought-after attitude of nostalgia. The delight we take in utilizing this elaborate approach is pure stagecraft, rooted in memorable romantic traditions and a deep love of classical proportions and detail. Beaux-Arts design expresses the academic Neoclassical style taught at the École Nationale Supérieure des Beaux-Arts in Paris in the seventeenth and eighteenth centuries. The school imprinted its classical Greek and imperial Roman aesthetic on the course of instruction, a course that continued during the Second Empire and the Third Republic that followed. In fact, Beaux-Arts instruction continued in Europe until the 1960s. In America, it was most popular from about 1880 to 1920 and became the style in which most of the important public buildings, libraries, universities, and residential structures of the era were designed.

Most interesting to me is that true neoclassical Beaux-Arts architecture, due to its use of proportions derived from the human body, symmetry, balance, and beauty, is pleasing to the eye no matter what one's personal taste is otherwise. The architecture and interiors incorporate sculptural decoration with impressionistic finish and realism, overscaled details, deep cornices, swags, and other sculptural enrichments, all in balance and proportion. In our Beaux-Arts–influenced projects, we adapt these flourishes and the use of symmetry and proportion to a modern discipline of restraint and harmony. We use the Beaux-Arts background as a "stage" or "set design" to which we add contemporary design elements or artworks that are of equal refinement, allowing the classical and the contemporary to work together in an intriguing, fresh manner.

Perhaps the pleasure of working within a Beaux-Arts style building, embellishing what is historic while adding in purely contemporary elements, comes from having fallen in love

with the elegant structures of the Museum of Fine Arts, Houston (MFAH).

The 1924 William Ward Watkin Neoclassical building on the South Lawn connects back-to-back with the 1958 and 1974 Ludwig Mies van der Rohe Modernist buildings on the North Lawn. Though the Modernist addition does not take stylistic cues from the Neoclassical, it carefully mimics the proportions, use of materials, and scale—almost as if the same hand made the two buildings, but with a different set of rules. The MFAH cemented my love for purity of design within a style and my appreciation for working in Neoclassical and Contemporary side by side.

I realized that architectural styles can beautifully accompany each other if the design is respectful of the delicate balance and does not overshadow it. This means that the designer does not try to downplay the ornate tradition or embellish the streamlined modern, which could instead result in a homogenized, bland work that reflects neither tradition nor advancement.

At Rottet Studio we enjoy the challenge of working with and manipulating historic styles, which offer a set of somewhat rigid parameters, to suit the project or existing structure. These Beaux-Arts projects provide inspiration, either enriching a design with a story steeped in the architectural and decorative framework of a romantic past or, conversely, presenting an opportunity to liberate the past through the marriage of the classical and the contemporary.

In either case, each of our Beaux-Arts works tells a story, which we recreate with a great respect for authenticity. We capture the essence of the historic style and display it in a fresh way. In fact, hidden lighting or focused lighting can add to the drama of historic fixtures. New proportions can emphasize paneling and molding. New materials made with new technologies can bring incredible richness, complexity, or simplicity to old historic forms and details.

CONTEMPORARY GRANDEUR

PRIVATE RESIDENCE

NEW YORK, NEW YORK

Some of the clients for whom we design both the "day home" (office) and the "night home" (private residence) reveal consistent aesthetic desires; others seek something very different from one space to another. In this case, when our client asked us to design his home in Manhattan, I was expecting it to be Contemporary, in keeping with the minimal Contemporary office design we had recently completed for his firm. When he told me it was in an early 1900s building with all of the original fireplaces, floors, and moldings, I realized that it was to be quite different from his "day home." As I walked into the space and was enveloped by the classically beautiful proportions, details, and materials, I fell in love with its character and charm. In my design, I retained and played off of the historic architecture but added contemporary furnishings and details and art that complemented and refreshed the historic elements.

A combination of two units, the home occupied a whole quadrant of the building, allowing us to create a formal living area, a family kitchen and living area, a bedroom zone for family, and a separate area for guests and visiting chefs. One of the wonderful aspects of designing this home was that the Ms. is a wonderful chef who cooks daily for the family. She left much of the design to me but was careful to specify all aspects of the kitchen, since she knew better than anyone what was needed. We selected a large Aga stove in eggplant and worked around it to provide a space that served as a kitchen for a true chef and also as a family room for after-school studying and preparing meals together.

The floor plan we devised preserved the historic grand rooms, focal vistas, and leaded-glass French doors, but created new bedroom suites and all-new bathrooms. We spent a great deal of time choosing the wall colors and researching what the fireplaces had originally looked like. Six different paint colors of white, gray, and beige were ultimately used, but all blend subtly together. Floors were refurbished and replicated in the exact manner of the original wood floors, and moldings were restored to their original state. The new bathrooms complement the historic French Beaux-Arts style and finish. Hand-painted wallpaper by de Gournay surrounds the dining room walls, and custom-designed églomisé panels flank the oversized leaded-glass doors between the dining room and the living room.

The furnishings are an eclectic combination of Old World reinterpreted and contemporary designer furniture, such as the Ralph Pucci chair that anchors the far corner of the living room. The couple had never pursued an art collection, so I encouraged them, as we needed significant art to accompany the furnishings and act as a foil to the Beaux-Arts decorative detail. I showed them a number of artists' works, but not until we began a discussion about how I love artists' drawings best did we land on our approach. My clients embraced the idea of a fine drawing collection and the loose free-form lines created when an artist is not pressured to perform but instead enjoys the process of drawing. This led the clients to purchase lovely drawings by Giacometti, Henry Moore, Matisse, and Picasso for the living room. For the foyer, we found an amazing Willem de Kooning drawing and a Robert Motherwell collage with drawing overlay. Other, larger-scale works and paintings are by Larry Poons, Zhang Huan, Richard Pousette-Dart, and Cleve Gray. A series of photographs by Alyson Shotz hangs in the corridor separating the kitchen from the living room, and a Kiki Smith resides over the family room's desk along with an Alfred Leslie painting and two Alyson Shotz line drawings. Works by Mark Wagner and Alex Katz also appear.

PREVIOUS PAGES: The living room of this New York residence mixes Old World culture and decorative detail with a modern flair, as seen through such elements as a cluster of modern artworks that includes drawings by Matisse, Giacometti, Henry Moore, and Picasso; a contemporary carpet of my design; and a low glass table. Open French doors lead to the kitchen.

RIGHT: Seen from the kitchen, the living room reveals large contemporary paintings by Cleve Gray and Larry Poons that share space with ornate Renaissance Revival details on the fireplace and ceiling.

A view from the dining room to the living room creates a regal impression of a classical enfilade multiplied in that room's central mirror. Flanking the doorway are panels with hand-painted de Gournay wallpaper and custom églomisé panels. A back-painted glass-topped dining table of my design reflects the classical surrounds.

ABOVE: In the front foyer with restored decorative wall paneling, a reception table designed by Eric Schmitt for Ralph Pucci sits beneath a chandelier from Circa Lighting. A Robert Motherwell acrylic, ink, and paper collage is complemented by four Alyson Shotz works in an adjacent hall.

OPPOSITE: The side entrance hall features a fanlight over-door transom window and a contemporary chandelier by Ted Abramczyk for Ralph Pucci. Muted colors, symmetry, and design restraint were used to focus attention on the historic building's structure.

LEFT: Pastel colors give the master bedroom a calm and peaceful appearance. A custom carpet, comfortably upholstered seating, the large mirror over the fireplace, and a simple four-poster bed add timeless elements to the design. A Richard Pousette-Dart painting and an Irving Penn photograph subtly dress the room.

ABOVE: The guest bedroom features charming hand-painted wallpaper by de Gournay depicting white birds nesting in tree branches.

CLASSIC REINTERPRETED

ROBERTO CAPUCCI

LOEWS REGENCY HOTEL

NEW YORK, NEW YORK

When Jon Tisch asked us to redesign the Loews Regency Hotel and help reposition it in its prestigious Park Avenue location, we were flattered and challenged, as this was a project personal to Jon and the entire Tisch family. Jon actually grew up in the hotel and knew it well. I've said before that when designing a hotel, I write a little script and assign to it characters through whose eyes I see. I never told Jon, but for the Loews Regency Manhattan, my character was him sitting back and smiling as he watched all the comings and goings of the hotel from the time he was a little boy until now. Though the façade of the building is a simple brick design, the lobby had always had a grand, luxurious presence. Given the location, clientele, and position of the hotel as the "power breakfast" place to be, we felt it appropriate to incorporate some of the design attitude of Beaux-Arts style—grand and classical, but with a twist. As well, Beaux-Arts–inspired moldings and paneling existed in many of the hotel's corridors and other areas and would have been cost prohibitive to completely remove. The renovation included the entry canopy, lobby, public spaces, meeting rooms, and guest rooms.

As I watched guests in the existing lobby for several days, I noticed that they always seemed so happy, smiling and even singing—twice I heard singing in the lobby: once it was Richard Simmons in what seemed to be a tutu, and another time, it was a group of shopping ladies in the elevator. Though a total transformation was in order, I knew we had to preserve the lively spirit that prevailed at the Regency. The idea of stage and theater kept coming to mind. With this hotel, the characters in my script—besides Jon—consisted of the happy people enjoying midtown Manhattan shopping, dining, and just strolling. There are subtle theatrical references in the new design, such as the curtain-like crenulated wall behind the front desk, which is made of expansive folding planes of high-gloss lacquered panels surrounded by an ornate chrome frame.

Other Beaux-Arts–inspired theatrical elements are evident in the pattern of the elevator lobby flooring, the sconces in the corridors, and the guest rooms' custom-designed entry and bedside lights. In the original lobby of the 1963 building, a seating group confronted visitors at the entrance and the front desk and back office support areas sat to the left. A redesign of the floor plan allowed us to open up the space to the right and create a hotel living room for sipping cocktails or reading and enjoying the Park Avenue scene.

We reclad the columns at the entry with gloss-lacquered and mirrored panels to reflect the surrounds, defying their size and acting as a portal framing the front desk. The lobby elevator doors were embellished with decorative metal paneling with an intricate pattern created by varying finish applications on the metal.

In the guest rooms, the theme of theatrical detail continues via a custom-designed wool carpet with intricate patterns held together by a softer oval shape. Giving special attention to the window wall—guests' first view upon entering the room—we designed luxurious drapery and shades and added high-gloss-painted faceted panels below the windows to enhance the visual movement and interest in the room. The furniture was all custom-designed in the vein of a residential bedroom. A leather headboard surrounds the bed on both sides, encompassing the bedside tables and conveying a feeling of ultra-luxurious bedding.

PREVIOUS PAGES: In the renovated double-height lobby at the historic Loews Regency Hotel in New York City, the front desk sits in front of a lacquer and chrome-plated decorative wall. The crenulations on the wall and desk reflect the outdoors, as well as guest movement. The entrance is complemented by custom chandeliers, desk, and wall treatments. Nearby, a private guest seating area at the back of the newly created guest lounge provides a quiet nook for social gatherings and evening cocktails.

RIGHT: An area to one side of the lobby features a quiet single-story space with a delightful wall overtaken by a tree art installation in relief pattern by Brooklyn artist Nina Helms.

HAUSSMANN'S PARIS REFLECTED

PAUL HASTINGS LLP

PARIS, FRANCE

Located in a historically significant early 1900s limestone building on Boulevard Haussmann in the 8th arrondissement, the Paris office of the law firm Paul Hastings is by far its most glamorous. We continued the theme of "endless space" reflected in the firm's other offices, but this time within a preservationist-protected environment. With Paul Hastings's Paris office, I began my exploration into designing within period architecture, reinterpreting the style through contemporary materials and details while preserving the characteristically gracious design of the original era. Unique to this project, the historic protection meant that many of the walls could not be reconfigured, so the design was focused on furniture, cabinetry, and the creative use of light, with a concentration on respectfully inserting new elements while reflecting the original details. Careful planning allowed for functional separation of public reception rooms from private practice areas within the historic fabric of the building. The furnishings are an eclectic combination of classic pieces and sleek custom consoles and conference tables and seating. A restrained palette of cream and dove-gray upholstery unifies everything, while a diverse range of textures and sheens creates visible depth and variety.

A historically significant treaty had been signed in the main boardroom, so we wanted to return it to its original state. The gilded walls and moldings as well as the chandeliers were restored. We custom designed a back-painted glass-top table; though purely contemporary, it strategically blended in with the room and literally reflected the period feel. We restored the endlessly spiraling staircase that appears to rise from the sunbathed lobby, added a built-in banquette at the window, and affixed an uplit dome over the minimal reception desk, which was also made to reflect its surroundings. The lighting design is a sophisticated blend of restored original fixtures, bespoke Murano chandeliers, concealed cove uplighting, and contemporary backlit glass elements.

Covering approximately 48,000 square feet spread among eight floors, this project was designed to accommodate 134 attorneys and staff, a conference floor, and a library. The primary materials used were those of the original structure—limestone, artisanal plaster, limed European oak, wrought iron, and glass. Through years of travel and visiting classically significant architecture, I had seen so many new, cold, contemporary, angular stainless-steel-and-glass spaces painfully forced into historic structures. I love the combination of glass and steel as materials but did not love the insensitive insertions. Years ago, I vowed that if I ever had the opportunity to design within one of these buildings, I would be more sensitive to their stature, a guiding principle through this project.

PREVIOUS PAGES: Classical drama consumes the lobby of the Paul Hastings offices in Paris, in the form of perfectly proportioned arches, marble columns, and a sweeping staircase complemented by a contemporary backlit glass and stainless steel reception desk meant to reflect, not distract from, the original space.

RIGHT: Gilded walls and chandeliers in the main conference room were preserved and restored to their original grandeur. Colored to match the classical room finishes, a contemporary custom-designed back-painted glass table reflects the ornate surroundings.

OPPOSITE: A corner of the entrance hall features a waiting area with a club chair by Antonio Citterio for Moroso and a custom low classical pedestal table of my design.

ABOVE LEFT: A tailored Moroso sofa with a light, floating appearance joins the seating group.

ABOVE RIGHT: In the managing partner's office, a desk of lacquered wood is lit by a French Deco lamp with a broad skirted base and a unique wing-like shade.

MOUNTAIN MANOR

CHESS MASTERPIECES
THE ALLURE OF MEN
LIVING ARCHITECTURE
HORSES MICHAEL EASTMAN

ST. REGIS ASPEN RESORT

ASPEN, COLORADO

For the St. Regis Aspen Resort, we conceptualized a quintessential Beaux-Arts mountain manor similar to what John Jacob Astor, the visionary behind the St. Regis brand, would have designed for the seasoned traveler during the Gilded Age: an uncompromising base for arbiters of fine food and wine, connoisseurs of culture, and adventure seekers. The interior and exterior renovation represents the new standard of luxury design in Aspen. The design blends historic elegance and tradition with the unpredictable addition of contemporary art and attitude, underscored by clever furnishings and accessories.

When I began traveling to Aspen to start the renovation design process, I would peruse local shops trying to better understand Aspen's culture. I quickly learned that everyone knew what was going on; they knew I was the designer slated to renovate the St. Regis, and everyone had a strong opinion about it. It was unanimous that I must not turn it into a contemporary hotel, as they had one of those, and I was to retain the warmth and tradition. With these orders in place thanks to numerous townspeople, I set out to affect a much-needed transformation that would still honor elements of the past. Designing in a traditional style does not preclude contemporary innovation—in fact, Astor was a known inventor, and certain elements of his homes were quite forward-thinking in his time.

We completely restructured the floor plan to allow for panoramic views of the mountain from anywhere in the hotel. Through the dark-metal-framed glass doors, the entry vestibule invites guests into a large, open Beaux-Arts reception area featuring a stunning mountain vista. The grand oval greeting table made of leather, embossed metal strapping, and amber onyx was designed in tandem with the overscaled embossed metal chandelier hanging above it. Set in front of the living room fireplace, the table and chandelier serve to provide a welcoming warm glow upon arrival and divert one's path to the front desk off to the right. Lobby furnishings were custom-designed to fit within the tapered window niches and to infuse the surroundings with a definitive mountain feel—as seen in the Austrian patterned hand-cast sabots on the sofas that flank the fireplace hearth and the sconces made of crystal lights hanging in front of embossed metal stanchions. The handwoven living room rug was conceived to organize the furniture and provide pattern where foot traffic was heavy.

We carefully selected colors that would lend warmth to the space and blend in with the natural colors of Aspen both in summer and in winter. I have learned that it is important to study the quality of light in a region, as it can vary greatly from one location to another—there's a particular tone to the light in Aspen that transforms the way we perceive a color, so we brought all of the finishes there to select on-site under the natural light.

For the corridors, my design team found historic etchings of mountains and had them re-created at such a large scale that it feels as though you are walking between the mountains. The effect is like going back in time to the 1880s, when Aspen was alive with the silver rush and Neoclassicism flourished. The guest rooms are a subtle blend of a suite in a historic late-nineteenth-century mountain manor and a contemporary home. Each has a mix of winter grays and warm summer tones, which connects the guest room with the striking outside views, and natural textures to create a rustic yet sophisticated environment. As everyone comes to Aspen to enjoy the refreshing outdoors year-round, antiqued mirrors were placed next to the windows so that as guests walk into the room, they literally see themselves outside.

PREVIOUS PAGES: To re-create the historical feeling of a Gilded Age manor, Rottet Studio drew on past Crafts traditions in elements such as the raised decorative felt wall by British artist Helen Amy Murray in a floral pattern, which sits behind the leather upholstered reception desk, and the traditional hand drawings of mountain landscapes that were enlarged to use as a wall covering.

RIGHT: Wood paneling, metal detailing, leather, and raw hide fabrics give life to the mountain experience in the Shadow Mountain Lounge, while large arched windows help connect guests with the outdoors through views of the majestic Aspen slopes.

My favorite feedback, relayed to me by the general manager of the hotel, was that many guests said they loved the new larger rooms. The rooms were exactly the same size! We had made them feel larger via the mirrors; a subtle manipulation of the ceiling moldings; the new, lighter colors; and the fact that we opened the bathrooms to the guest room with paneled doors. We incorporated antiqued oak flooring with a warm, dark stain overlaid with a delicate whitewash. An accent rug added additional warmth. Each room was detailed with custom furnishings including a leather bed and desk designed by Ralph Lauren and a unique faux-shagreen chest of drawers and side tables. Leather-wrapped sconces, which send light up and down, were created for bedside and bathroom. All of the marble-clad bathrooms feature hand-cast stainless-steel vanities with Neoclassical details and dual sinks. Careful attention was given to the lighting throughout the space, especially in the bathrooms, where we have perfected how to illuminate the room so a guest can see clearly while shaving or putting on makeup.

In a hallway passage carpeted in manor-house fashion, a long nineteenth-century-style sofa plays off a whimsical wallpaper of overscale flowers and credenzas piled high with bulbous vases made of ceramic and metals.

The Astor Library features a cozy cluster of low wing chairs and comfortable sofas before a mellow fireplace. Lighting from sconces and ceiling lights, as well as recessed downlights, gives the room a romantic character. The carpet is a custom design of mine.

ABOVE: Guest suites have traditional elegance with leather headboards, side draperies, and custom sconces. The dog portraits were drawn by my sister, Lynda Wood, who is an artist and an art teacher.

OPPOSITE, ABOVE & OPPOSITE, BELOW LEFT: Suites feature a custom-designed desk with a leather saddlebag to hold the hotel's compendium and guest reference books.

OPPOSITE, BELOW RIGHT: Offering a natural look and texture, faux shagreen covers the drawers of this custom chest of drawers of my design. Drawer pulls are wrapped leather.

ABOVE: Accommodating guests with luxurious soaking tubs is a manor-house tradition and one I drew upon for each suite and for each guest needing some spa time after hours on the slopes. Double doors offer views of the mountains and help expand the space.

RIGHT: Light gray marble lines the walls and floor in the guest baths. An inset cast stainless steel vanity counter with double sinks was designed to appear as a freestanding console.

Nº 20

HONORING
COCO

THE SURREY HOTEL

NEW YORK, NEW YORK

The Surrey Hotel is a special project, as it launched Rottet Studio into the fascinating world of hotel design. I had not designed a hotel since the early 1990s Solana Marriott, where Ricardo Legorreta was the architect and I was the interior designer. In the interim, I had been focusing on office design, but I had thousands of hotel design ideas stored in the back of my mind. The stars aligned when Patrick Denihan, hotelier and owner of the Surrey, reached out to us through my New York partner, David Davis. The Surrey is in a historically protected 1926 Beaux-Arts building at the corner of 76th and Madison, and Denihan was seeking a fresh, refined contemporary approach to Beaux-Arts.

At the beginning of the conceptual phase, I stayed at the hotel for a few days, listening to the sounds of Upper East Side mornings, evenings, and nights and watching the activities, habits, and haunts of the local community. Our client gave me E. B. White's book *Here Is New York* and said, "It will help you understand the city." I read it while staying at the Surrey, and a design story began to unfold. I decided that instead of the large-scale lobby that had been previously drawn, the lobby should be returned to its intimate size, as in the finer Beaux-Arts pied-à-terre buildings of the neighborhood. I envisioned Coco Chanel living here, entering the lobby late in the evening, throwing her coat on the sofa, and telling the doorman to take it up for her, as she was going to the bar for a martini. Then I realized that the existing program did not call for a bar, so the next morning I phoned our client to tell them we needed a bar for two reasons: (1) It would give the guests someplace to sit while waiting to be seated at the hotel's restaurant, Café Boulud, and (2) Coco needed one. He approved of the idea, though he did not understand the second reason until I presented the concept a few weeks later.

I began to see the hotel design as if it were the stage for a new movie filmed and directed in the style of classic Chanel—in black and white. From that point on, I looked at the design as if through a black-and-white lens since black-and-white photography romances history, making even the plainest of people and environments undeniably alluring. Like a director, I began to imagine what appeared before the actor's stage right and stage left, where he or she would sit and stand, and how the scenes would unfold. The Surrey Hotel was the beginning of my exploration into storytelling through interior design.

The hotel is subtle and sophisticated yet rich with intrigue and style. A closer look into the design, however, reveals that classical, traditional details and materials have been used in a contemporary manner and reinterpreted to give the illusion of nostalgia without the staidness. Instead of using an antique Oriental rug that would have been in the lobby in the 1920s, for example, we created a black-and-white "rug" made of marble mosaic and skewed its proportions to be more surrealist than classic. Recessed elongated star-shaped lights hover above in the ceiling at the elevator lobby, subtly indicating where to go to find "sleep."

I also wanted the hotel to have an art collection that was completely contemporary and curated with a similar point of view to that of the design—a reinterpretation of classical beauty. Behind the front desk, I placed two Jenny Holzer photographs of poems written through projections on classically designed buildings in Venice. The photographs naturally fit into the classical proportions and the black-and-white mood, even though Jenny Holzer is far from classical. At the focal point from the front door leading to the elevators, I placed a Chuck Close tapestry of Kate Moss, a portrait of Kate in her most natural state, revealing her facial moles and flaws—some

PREVIOUS PAGES: "A home away from home for Coco Chanel" was the design theme that inspired the renovation of Manhattan's iconic Upper East Side hotel The Surrey. In the entrance lobby, guests are greeted by an oversized portrait of model Kate Moss by artist Chuck Close.

OPPOSITE: Photographs by Jenny Holzer hang behind the reception desk, a reminder of the art, culture, and social standing of the hotel and another homage to Coco Chanel, who probably would have appreciated the beautiful images of the forward-thinking Holzer.

YOU ARE MY OWN

find it intriguingly beautiful, and others question it. In either case, it is captivating and emotionally arresting, as true art is intended to be. Claes Oldenburg's huge and fanciful shoelace hangs in the lobby, and my favorite work—video art by William Kentridge—is embedded in the foyer leading to the bar. The guests stop and watch as the pages of a book are turned and eventually reveal the figure of a woman, but just as one catches sight of her, she disappears.

The lobby bar, Bar Pleiades, was intentionally designed for the contemporary version of Coco Chanel and her friends holding court: talking, plotting, and laughing into the evening with martinis and fine wine in hand. Since the building was built in what was considered the last year for Beaux-Arts style and the beginning of Art Deco, I created the bar to appear as if it had been introduced to the hotel in the late 1920s, at the high point of Deco, before Prohibition. We made the space elegant yet warm and engaging, with seating areas inside large black angular lacquer boxes with inlaid white lines inspired by the simplicity and beauty of Coco Chanel's compacts, as captured in a black-and-white photograph. Seen from the front, the shape emulates a set where the curtains have been pulled back to reveal the excitement onstage, represented by the warm beige suede tufted walls, white sharkskin seating, and patrons enjoying themselves. The enclosed banquette seating allows guests to be seen displaying their fashions yet protects their conversations, adding to the intrigue.

A hand-painted de Gournay mural of India during the early years of American travel is hung above the classically designed sofas on the opposite side of the bar. This intentional nod to the early 1920s, when the hotel was first opened, reflects the layers of time and influence found in historic places such as New York's Upper East Side. The Surrey has been selected as *Condé Nast Traveler*'s number one hotel in New York City since its inception in 2009.

In the lobby, a hand-laid marble mosaic floor replaces the predictable Oriental rug. Warm-colored limestone; black, gray, and white Carrara marble; and a faux skylight articulate the classical yet modern design of the newly renovated space.

ABOVE: Shelves clustered with candles (lit at precisely six o'clock every evening) in a corner of the lobby define the sense of luxury and romance of The Surrey.

RIGHT: A tufted sofa and club chairs by Moroso enliven the space, where leaded glass offers exposure to natural light from the street through the entry vestibule yet enough privacy for conversation.

RICHARD SERRA

NTRAL PA
LUNGED
VED ALO
NG THE T

OPPOSITE: Bar Pleiades at The Surrey features “box stages” inspired by Coco Chanel and framed by angled walls that resemble pulled-back curtains awaiting a unique play defined by their inhabitants.

ABOVE, LEFT: The counter at the bar is a stage set all its own. Using my sketches, Jimmie Martin hand-painted graffiti on the back of the bar-stools for a classic yet edgy look.

ABOVE, RIGHT: Bar Pleiades has areas of café seating, where the focus is on the custom carpet. Marked with stencil-like graffiti messages for Coco and the bar patrons, it captures the feeling of many of The Surrey’s contemporary artworks.

LEFT: The main bedroom within the Presidential Suite is predominantly white with a custom-designed carpet in a dark, whimsical pattern, evoking the feeling of being in a black-and-white movie.

ABOVE: The living room of the Presidential Suite offers a chaise, sofa, and chairs comfortably grouped around a fireplace. The balcony door and double-hung windows give access to the Upper East Side view.

PRINTS
Catalogue raisonné
ESTAMPES

CHERRY

nestled

OPPOSITE, CLOCKWISE FROM ABOVE LEFT: Demonstrating a bit of artistic license, contemporary nostalgic details that might be discovered by a Coco of today include books featuring the works of Richard Serra; the recipe for a Manhattan cocktail hand-drawn by artist Jimmie Martin on a chaise longue; armoire hardware with tassel pulls; and poems written by me and printed on the cushions of banquettes in the guest room.

ABOVE, CLOCKWISE FROM LEFT: The bathroom sconce was custom designed with an Art Deco flair; an antique armoire was overtaken by poetic script and bold graffiti by artist Jimmie Martin; art books and "hand-drawn" details dress the tabletop.

ABOVE: The entrance to the spa features custom-designed carpet and a hand-laid glass mosaic wall feature.

RIGHT: At the spa, a marble sink takes on rich carved details. To emphasize the color scheme and define the shapes, white subway tile has dark-hued grout. Decorative "tube" lighting, the subway tile, and the marble bath provide a sense of luxury that fits the retro style while still maintaining the contemporary amenities.

LEFT: Resembling that of an Upper East Side residence, the dining room of the penthouse features a Meridian chandelier and a coffered ceiling. Separating the dining area from the living area with its fireplace is a custom-designed Deco-style credenza by Impressions Architectural Millwork, which contrasts with the Twisted Vine floor lamp by Neiman Marcus. Dining chairs with custom graffiti-style backs echo the set style of the romantic Bar Pleiades downstairs.

ABOVE: On the étagère with a modern geometric shelf arrangement are candles and books that elevate style to the level of art, including those paying homage to a Coco Chanel-inspired scene with a social and stylish flair, such as *Vanity Fair Portraits*.

BEAUX-ARTS:
EXPLORATIONS IN CLASSICAL PROPORTIONS

When a space is restrictive in size or height, I consider incorporating classical design and proportions to deceive the eye. For a hotel in San Francisco (right, above and below), I manipulated classical Beaux-Arts techniques to create the illusion of a more expansive space. A high-gloss ceiling soffit reflects and vertically expands the bronze wall below and offers the illusion of height, and the rotating ceiling planes in the entry defy the low ceiling. The circular lobby space spirals off the entry like a Pythagorean curve leading to the lounge area and beyond. For the conceptual design of a historic resort (above), I utilized formal classical planning and details layered with contemporary forms and furniture.

KOLOMAN MOSER
KOLOMAN MOSER
DONALD JUDD
SKIN LAURENT ELIE BADESSI

MEDITERRANEAN

To work in contemporary Mediterranean design is to celebrate the gracious yet casual indoor-outdoor lifestyle of today. It is also an opportunity to reinterpret what makes the Mediterranean style so comfortable and coveted: natural warm materials that are of the earth, such as weathered limestone, deep natural woods intertwining with organic plant materials, or sunlight filtering in through deep recessed windows that give the feeling of protection while being of the elements. This aesthetic calls for the use of ornament in a dignified, refined way, as moments of visual pleasure that are authentic to the materials of today and not applied in a faux manner. With these tools and principles, I strive to create an environment that is specific to its circumstances yet rich with the emotional pleasures of historic Mediterranean architecture.

As a popular style, Mediterranean Revival was introduced in the United States in the late nineteenth century. It included various references from Spanish Renaissance, Spanish Colonial, Italian Renaissance, and Venetian Gothic architecture, along with formal elements from other European countries, such as France, Greece, Portugal, and the Balkans. Decorative metal, tile, and wood elements also came from North African countries like Tunisia, Morocco, and Algeria. The movement gained popularity during the 1920s and

’30s, and resurged in the 1960s, drawing on the residential style of palaces and seaside villas, which worked well for the coastal resorts and houses of California, Florida, and the southern states with climates similar to that of the Mediterranean region. Basic features of Mediterranean Revival design are rectangular floor plans; massive primary façades with decorated door surrounds; stucco walls; red tile roofs; arches for windows, doors, porticoes, or arcades; wood or wrought-iron balconies; and window grilles. Lush gardens with reflecting pools and fountains often accompany these structures, and Mediterranean designs may feature terraces or courtyards. Ornamental details range from large wooden doors with ornate carvings, sculpted-stucco or carved-stone detail, intricate metal-and-glass chandeliers and sconces, and wood or tile floors to patterned, multicolored tiles defining doors, windows, fountains, or the risers of staircases and pavers of terraces.

The allure of Tuscany and the South of France has tugged at me often while I have enjoyed many summer and winter vacations in classic Mediterranean architecture such as Villa d’Este on Lake Como. The memories of Villa d’Este were strong contributors to the design of The Beverly Hills Hotel Presidential Bungalows, where we sought to create the ultimate California Mediterranean luxury in true bungalow style.

More recently, a stay at Palacio Belmonte in Lisbon, a fifteenth-century palace restored and converted to a boutique hotel, stole my heart and influenced my design. I was struck by the way the palace and its owner were like instrument and musician. Carefully playing the architectural elements—opening and closing perfectly placed windows to allow a magical dance of light throughout the day; setting a pot of lavender in view; placing warm bread and preserves out by morning; and, in the evening, opening 200-year-old carved wooden doors in the corridors to reveal deep, candle-lit plaster niches filled with crystal and scotch—the owner set a stage of intrigue, romance, and deep comfort. Both the palace and its owner taught me how to captivate a guest through gracious architectural moves, the use of light, and lovingly set moments of enjoyment—simple, perfect.

These memories became reality in several of our recent projects: The Four Seasons Casa Medina in Bogotá, Colombia, a historic Spanish Colonial building; a contemporary Mediterranean home in Santa Monica set around a courtyard; and my first ground-up house in my hometown of Houston. The elements of Mediterranean style are as valid today as ever because they are based on creating architecture that coexists with the natural elements of the land and climate.

WINCHELL
NEAL GABLER

LUXURIOUS BUNGALOW

The

THE BEVERLY HILLS HOTEL PRESIDENTIAL BUNGALOWS

BEVERLY HILLS, CALIFORNIA

An addition to the historic Beverly Hills Hotel, originally designed by Elmer Grey in the Mediterranean Revival style in 1912, offered the opportunity for a from-the-ground-up architecture and interior design project. Hidden by foliage, the original façade actually features a Mission-style gable, typical of the eighteenth-century Spanish missions that were the first grand architectural feats in the region. A century later, in 2012, we completed two new bungalows where two tennis courts had existed. We finished the exteriors of the Presidential Bungalows, as they were dubbed, in the peachy pink and green trim colors that have become a trademark of the hotel and its iconic Polo Lounge.

These two new "ultra bungalows" offer the comfort and privacy of private residences along with the service and attention to detail for which the "Pink Palace" is so widely renowned. To fit the Mediterranean character of the property, the bungalows have tile roofs, intimate gardens, and the famous pink stucco that gives the hotel its nickname, and each Presidential Bungalow offers guests a blend of traditional and modern design, with warm, casual California elegance throughout.

Each bungalow comprises 1,500 square feet of outdoor living space and 3,500 square feet indoors, including three bedrooms, a great room/dining room with full kitchen, a study, and five fireplaces. Individually keyed bedrooms with access via a private courtyard assure maximum flexibility. Though the suites are the ultimate in luxury accommodation, they are comfortable, casual, and cozy, not glitzy or overdecorated, and in keeping with Old Hollywood's passion for the bungalow style. There are hand-distressed walnut floors and luxurious custom rugs throughout, with hand-troweled plaster and vaulted ceilings to frame the scene. Living in Los Angeles for fourteen years, I cherished indoor and outdoor fireplaces to warm the crisp, cool evenings year-round, and thus I provided each bungalow with five interior and two exterior fireplaces made of hand-carved limestone. Most of the furniture, including the beds, end tables, coffee tables, sofas, and entry table, was custom designed by Rottet Studio specifically for the bungalows and made by local California craft shops, some of which had been in business since the hotel was built. The custom bathroom vanities, reminiscent of the famed palm branches, were also made locally.

Expansive sliding glass doors lead to each bungalow's private pool and the living and dining areas in the outdoor courtyard, letting in glorious California sunshine when the doors are open or closed. Each bungalow has its own secure, private garden with soundproof walls to ensure comfort and serenity.

PREVIOUS PAGES: For the Beverly Hills Hotel's Presidential Bungalows, Rottet Studio designed, built, and furnished two new structures where two tennis courts had originally existed. Each of the 3,500-square-feet bungalows offers outdoor living space, a key ingredient in any Mediterranean design.

RIGHT: Seen through the sliding glass doors, the pink stucco walls of the hotel were continued for each new bungalow, offering privacy for each pool and the perfect color to complement the live garden wall. Exposed-beam ceilings give way to hand-scraped walnut floors and cut-out pattern sheer drapes hang in front of solid ones, giving the bungalow a casual feel.

LEFT: A grand traditional fireplace suits the Mediterranean sensibility and warms the master bedroom of each bungalow suite. A slightly recessed and indirectly lit wall adds prominence to the custom bed and side tables, from which one can control the lighting, temperature, and sound system for the entire bungalow.

ABOVE: The upholstered headboard tapers to visually embrace each bedside table. A lamp by Arteriors casts a parabola on the inset wall panels covered with Bart Halpern fabric.

OPPOSITE: Beams from the raised ceiling add dimension to the living room, where the focal fireplace is crowned with artwork by Claes Oldenburg. The large framed mirror to its right echoes the window on its left. Finished with a custom Rottet Studio design rug by Tai Ping, this eclectic mix of furnishings is a hallmark of contemporary California Mediterranean style.

ABOVE: The casual den of the bungalow features an extraordinary wall covering by Élitis depicting the Torrey Pines State Natural Reserve, which captures the feeling of being surrounded by nature. Hexagonal-top nesting tables with macassar veneer and black lacquer legs and the wraparound sectional sofa were envisioned to tuck together.

Colombia
Luis Roldán

ROMANTIC COLONIAL

FOUR SEASONS CASA MEDINA

BOGOTÁ, COLOMBIA

For the Four Seasons Casa Medina in Bogotá, we preserved the Mediterranean beauty of the original redbrick building while introducing modern elements and renovating the newer wing into a seamless extension of the historic property. The boutique hotel had been a single-family home built in the 1940s, later converted into a hotel with a building added at the time of conversion. The project presented a specific set of challenges and offered a host of rewards in our first foray into Central/South America. I found Bogotá to have a fantastically dynamic and deep culinary and artistic thread; we sought to emulate that creativity and richness in our design.

The story I imagined for this lovely little hotel in the heart of Bogotá's historic area began with a vision of the lush green, foggy environment of the Andes Mountains, the petite brick building covered in ivy, and the Spanish Colonial–style architecture. I remembered the scene from *Mr. and Mrs. Smith* when they were supposedly in Colombia, and the romantic environment is portrayed through colors: fuchsia, emerald green, and gold seen through a moody lens. The historic building was perfect in character except for the nonconforming additions that had been tacked on to it over the years. We sought to remove those and bring back the original character throughout the space, but we also wanted to add in some unexpected contemporary design elements that would pique the guests' interest and emphasize that Bogotá is not really a Spanish colonial city anymore; instead, it is a city of great culinary treats, art, and crafts, as well as a major financial center.

To that end, we researched local crafts, artists, building practices, and cultural references to balance the house's honored heritage with the right amount of freshness, contemporary style, and Four Seasons amenities. Structurally, the building posed challenges due to the solid masonry walls and the property's status as a historic national monument to which any changes required prior approval by a city council committee. As well, each room was a different type, so it became like designing a custom home with eighty-one bedrooms, each with unique features such as fireplaces and hand-carved wooden beam ceilings. In one of the suites there is a tiny door in the corner under the stair—no more than 30 inches tall and leading to nowhere—a true remnant of Spanish Colonial architecture, with its mystery and allure.

As with most projects, the interior design began at the exterior entry, so the landscaping we used for the property's entry gave it a manicured Four Seasons look, instantly signaling to arriving guests that they are in a pristine, well-appointed venue. We restored the original brick and plaster entry hall, replaced the anachronistic and intrusive chandelier, and set a proper foyer table under the new focal chandelier. The reception area to the left of the entry was small with the receptionist set behind a walled-in room, which did not offer a friendly or welcoming first impression. We opened the whole reception area up to allow a view of the lovely ivy-covered courtyard, increased the size for a more luxurious feel, then created a custom hand-carved millwork ceiling and a somewhat whimsical front desk that exemplifies the Colombian craft of intricate wood carving. The sitting room to the right of the entry corridor was transformed into a hotel lounge with power and data connections so guests could do a bit of work while mingling.

PREVIOUS PAGES: The entrance to the 1940s brick and stone Four Seasons Hotel Casa Medina reflects the unique flavor of Spanish Mediterranean style found in Bogotá, Colombia. Its South American accent authentically captures the essence of gracious indoor-outdoor living and respect for natural materials.

OPPOSITE: With references to the Moorish-inspired woodworking that impacted Spanish Mediterranean style, the original wood paneling in the Casa Medina's reception area was supplemented by contemporary Bogotá wood-carvers, providing a striking backdrop for the reception desk of my design.

ABOVE: Spanish Colonial–style chairs of wood and tooled leather flank a stately painting in a similar vernacular.

OPPOSITE: A unique rope handrail makes nautical allusions. Bogotá is inland, but all of Colombia is adjacent to the Caribbean Sea, and many Colombians embrace carefree coastal style and nautical imagery.

As with many Spanish Colonial and Mediterranean buildings, this one was set around a courtyard perfectly aged and lush with ivy and vegetation, so it already exuded the very romantic character many people try to reproduce. Because the courtyard was critical to the overall ambiance of the hotel, we conceived the new courtyard restaurant and bar to be of similar Old World character. Nestled in front of the lush ivy-covered wall, the new hotel bar features historic mosaic floor tiles that were painstakingly maintained, as well as the natural red brick surrounding the columns and walls that defined the courtyard space. The restaurant designer, Saúl Sasson of Bogotá, realized this concept in his well-executed design utilizing handmade floor tiles and adding even more greenery to the walls.

We spent a great deal of time analyzing the existing art and antiques in order to find locations where their authentic beauty could be appreciated. New pieces were curated from art galleries and artists' studios to complement and intentionally contrast with the existing artwork for a contemporary nod. All of the artwork featured in the hotel is by Colombian artists or artists currently living in Colombia. After using much of the existing antique furniture in the guest corridor lobbies, we again relied heavily on local artisans and vendors—almost all of the case goods, drapery, millwork, and metalwork were made or sourced in Bogotá. This was done not only to circumvent the time lost in importing goods but also to infuse each space with regional character.

OPPOSITE: Deep-stained wood beams and smaller vigas contrast with the white walls and give the ceiling of the Casa Medina guest rooms a medieval appearance, something often associated with Mediterranean residential style.

ABOVE: Every nook was utilized for the guests. A writing desk with modern lines faces outward to the floor-to-ceiling view of foliage and landscaping.

ABOVE: The interior courtyard is a private, vine-covered outdoor room enclosed by the property's rusticated stone and brick façade. A brick fireplace warms the space at night, while decorative local Spanish Colonial–style tiles pave the courtyard floor. Other local materials include the yellow-hued stones and red brick.

OPPOSITE: Connected to the courtyard is the hotel bar, designed by Bogotá architect Saúl Sasson. A live garden wall flourishes beneath a retractable glass atrium ceiling strung with lights so guests can party into the night and under the stars.

castañyoles
castañyoles

SOUTHERN CALIFORNIA LIVING

LIBRARIES
ISSEY MIYAKE
TASCHEN

CROFT RESIDENCE

SANTA MONICA, CALIFORNIA

In true Mediterranean style, this home is anchored around an intimate courtyard patio, which features lovely gardens, a specimen tree, a fireplace, and a lap pool. During the day, sunlight beams through the house, and almost every room extends into this magical outdoor space through glass patio doors. In the evening, the garden lights illuminate the scene, and the patio transforms into a dramatic backdrop for the interiors, offering true Mediterranean indoor-outdoor living.

Though the floor plan was excellent, the existing home required a full exterior and interior renovation. The architecture of the home slightly echoes that of Frank Lloyd Wright's early Los Angeles homes with its cubic forms and warm sand-colored, brick-washed elevations. The volumes are reminiscent of the work of Richard Neutra, but it is a perfect example of Mediterranean style in the way the house opens itself up to the outside with leaded-glass doors giving way to the sun-drenched courtyard.

The new owners had spent many memorable evenings in this home when it belonged to their good friends Tanis and Bill McGregor, and had always loved the way it flowed. We maintained most aspects of the original house—the floor plan and layout, the existing concrete floors, the glass windows and doors, and the natural brick façade—and, to accommodate our client's needs, we added a second-floor gym and office with a separate entry from a new set of back stairs.

As the project went forward, the owners decided to remodel the kitchen to make it a bit more formal and refined. This was done with Calacatta Gold stone countertops, glass tile, and the stainless-steel counters around the new Wolf stove. Skylights were placed in the master suite, and the bathroom was completely remodeled with white back-painted glass cabinets and a Nublado travertine floor and countertops. The impeccable custom-designed lighting was inspired by our hotel experience. When remodeling and repurposing all of the other rooms for our empty-nester clients, we kept visiting family and friends front of mind. The Ms.'s dressing room and closet were appointed with white back-painted glass cabinet doors, a Jean de Merry chest of drawers, a custom handwoven rug, and a vintage chandelier from the couple's Brentwood home. The husband's dressing area was made of a figured Cerejeira wood, masculine but refined.

Leaded-glass French doors open from the kitchen, living room, and family room onto the courtyard. A custom Martin Pierce ping-pong table takes center stage in the family room as the Mr. was a champion ping-pong player at USC.

Inside, the house transforms itself into a California expression of simple elegance and sophistication. As my design associate Laurence Cartledge says: "It's a house that allows its owners to relax with family and celebrate with friends. The furniture and finish selection is a personal reflection of the clients' chic and simple tastes." The rug and the fabrics in the living room were selected to complement the Candida Höfer photograph that overlooks the space. We loved the idea of having this grand image of a Renaissance library in juxtaposition with the two-story library and mezzanine that anchors the back of the room.

The guest bedroom, just off the entry hall and opposite the living room, needed to be elevated in its design and finishes since the clients planned to use it for coat storage and possibly as a ladies' lounge during parties. Here, the Fromental silk wall covering offers a scenic delight of birds, flowers, and trees, and there is a moment of enchantment and humor in the bedpost finials carved as small wooden birds. While this is a modern, casual California home, many of the Renaissance-inspired artworks and decorative elements, like these finials, correspond to traditional realistic decorations typical of the Mediterranean style. Custom-designed glass églomisé panels surround the dining room window on the street side, while the opposite side opens to prime courtyard views. The design of this home was a true collaboration of the owners; their friend and interior designer Catherine Bailly Dunne; the original architect and the home's previous owner, their friend Bill McGregor; and Rottet Studio.

PREVIOUS PAGES: The double-height living room with exposed brick, structural steel, and a grid wall of glass opens to the courtyard in true Mediterranean style.

RIGHT: The living room is showered with indirect light. The fireplace acts as a substantial visual anchor of the design, while a large artwork by Candida Höfer gives the room a distinctive presence and adds to the Mediterranean spirit. The mezzanine above holds the couple's library, which spills over from the bookshelves below.

With a lap pool, fireplace, dining area, and specimen olive tree, the exterior courtyard pays homage to California outdoor living. From morning through evening, the family can enjoy the sun-drenched courtyard while nestling by the living room fireplace, preparing meals in the kitchen, or playing ping-pong in the family room. The dark metal window grid and exposed steel beams complement the fireplace's smooth concrete texture and the exterior brickwork while maintaining clear modern forms.

PREVIOUS PAGES: The kitchen offers an elegant dining nook with a Calacatta Gold marble tabletop, matching the slab kitchen countertops. Rich white oak wood cabinetry surrounds the space, and the classic Wolf stove's stainless steel hood, while large, is no rival to the vintage glass chandelier selected by Catherine Bailly Dunne.

OPPOSITE: Well lit by a broad skylight, the spacious master bedroom is nearly double height. The walls are predominantly silk-wrapped panels, and the fabric's warm hue is echoed in the drapery and cornice at the glass wall connected to the balcony and open courtyard. A custom carpet by Odegard adds softness underfoot.

ABOVE: The bedside table of my design with Sherbert Wagner hardware was conceived with the ultimate respect for craftsmanship and design simplicity.

MEDITERRANEAN REDEFINED

STOLLE RESIDENCE

HOUSTON, TEXAS

When Kevin Stolle asked me to design his home in the heavily wooded Memorial district of Houston, I was thrilled, as I had not yet designed a home from the ground up. I told him that if he loved the characteristic comfortable indoor-outdoor feel of the Mediterranean style but could live without the faux arches and terra-cotta tile roof, we could compose a home of warm, Old World materials that was truly contemporary at the same time and fit for his lifestyle with his two sons.

As I do when designing hotels, I wrote a story about the "history" of the home and its ultimate aesthetic. The weathered limestone of Mediterranean style was appropriate for the ground planes, as stone is of the earth and has truly been there forever. So I composed all of the foundations, courtyard walls, and paths leading to and around the home out of limestone and crushed granite. I imagined the home to have originally been made of two stone structures that over time were connected by a metal and glass annex and that these structures were "wrapped" in a new contemporary plaster façade to protect them.

We created a surrounding landscape that is an extension of the home. Memorial Drive is a lovely but busy street that links west and east Houston, so I wanted to set the home back from it, true to Mediterranean style. We composed a layering of walls and courts: The first wall is ivy-covered and serves to soften the visual approach as well as dampen sound from the street to the home. The second wall is composed of rough limestone rock partially covered with smooth plaster. A reinterpreted Mediterranean gate leads to another courtyard separating the front door of the home from the drive court. This series of limestone walls continues visually through the home into the expansive backyard, where we employed Renaissance landscape notions—the idea of forced perspective—by angling in the walls to give the yard an even longer appearance. At the rear of the property, we created what seems like an infinite horizon by introducing a topographic berm at the rear property line separating the yard and pool area from a sunken dog run.

A crushed-granite driveway borders the exterior of the house, leading to a three-car garage with an extensive workbench for repair of all types of mechanical devices (bikes, motorbikes, vintage cars, and Jet Skis, to name a few). The prize vintage car sits above on a lift so it is on display but protected.

The residence is 10,000 square feet with five bedrooms, five bathrooms, and two half bathrooms. Inside, we wanted each room to have a unique vantage point of an outdoor space. The main living room looks directly onto the pool and has a view over the entire back lawn, whereas the dining room focuses on the front courtyard view over olive trees, ivy-covered limestone walls, and a koi pond with flowering water lilies. On the west side, the kitchen is situated next to a culinary garden, ripe with vegetables and other assorted produce. To the south, the kitchen looks over the family room with an extended view to the outdoor living area and fireplace. Featuring a stainless-steel La Cornue stove, matching appliances, and custom oak millwork, the kitchen has an Old World Mediterranean feeling. All the woodwork in the kitchen was constructed with two-hundred-year-old farmhouse oak beams, also utilized in the outdoor pool house, granting the home the rustic charm of a Mediterranean villa. The ground-floor bedrooms have accessible courtyards surrounded by lavender, ivy, and other Mediterranean plants. The library opens onto a serene courtyard on the east side, with a lush, quiet garden and a tranquility fountain made from a vintage limestone water trough from the South of France. The study looks onto the pool, the outdoor fireplace, and the two-story limestone wall that serves as the outdoor movie wall. The home is situated to allow in the natural breezes from the southwest during the spring, fall, and winter, when the Houston climate is less severe.

Large steel-framed windows with curtains allow for as little or as much light as is desired in an open living room area with an unbroken view of the backyard pool and surrounding

PREVIOUS PAGES: Aspects of Mediterranean architecture were used for this residence in order to allow its inhabitants to enjoy the textures and forms of centuries-old traditions. Tall glass walls in the living room invite in the garden view and bring in the light year-round. Glass and mirror reflections capture more views in unexpected locations.

OPPOSITE: Exterior and interior views merge almost seamlessly with a painting by Joe Mancuso as the focal point at the end of the hallway.

acreage. To the left of the entrance door, a grand staircase with a custom steel railing overlooks the entrance hall and double-height living room. To the left of the living room is a cozy library with floor-to-ceiling custom millwork and a wood-coffered ceiling. To the right of the double-height living room, the dining area is flanked by a double-sided marble-clad fireplace on one side and a glass wine storage wall on the other.

The grand entrance staircase leads up to the second-story living quarters, as well as a 500-square-foot game-and-media room, and the third-floor roof terrace with a reclaimed oak trellis and a fire pit. Above the master bedroom, a private roof garden takes advantage of the city views and an elevation at which the night breezes cool it even in the heat of summer. Upstairs bedrooms were selected by the various family members based on their favorite view. The spacious master suite includes a master bath flanked by custom carved-stone door frames and herringbone marble flooring.

The transparency and interconnection of the main home and pool house speak to Stolle's desire that the property feel both intimate and expansive, Old World and contemporary. Visible from the grand living room windows, the rear pool is bordered with four-inch-thick limestone. It is accompanied by an indoor-outdoor living room/pool house with kitchen elements, a fireplace, and entertainment media, including a television hidden behind a vintage wood panel that raises up with a mechanical pull, a feature designed by our engineer client. Made of reclaimed wood beams and reclaimed light gray clay tile roofing and limestone, the pool house is historic as an extension of the limestone foundation, which, in the story I invented for the design of this house, reflects what "Old World" truly means. In keeping with my passion for authentic historic or distinctly contemporary design, we preserved the richness of classic Mediterranean architecture without resorting to faux-Mediterranean motifs.

In the Stolle residence, the living room and its transparency to the outdoors are paramount. Beyond the modern yet traditional furnishings and rich materials of stone, marble, and glass is the pool terrace, a rise of green grass, and a pool house with its own terrace at right.

KOLOMAN MOSER
Willem de Kooning

PREVIOUS PAGES: On axis with the living room seating and fireplace is an inviting view to a quaint side courtyard with a vintage limestone trough fountain from the South of France. The painting is by Joe Mancuso. Side tables with antiqued bronze, glass, and a linen drape were custom designed by Rottet Studio, as was the carpet produced by Sacco.

RIGHT: Dappled light from the side courtyard filters into the study with its large-scale openings both to the outside and in, to the living room. With floor-to-ceiling bookcases and cabinetry, the room is imbued with the warmth of the stained oak.

PORTRAITS
LUXURY TOYS FOR MEN

OPPOSITE & ABOVE: The homeowner requested a kitchen with an Old World feel. The dimensions of the high-ceilinged space and the recycled wood deliver on that design promise. A view from the free-standing counter to the stove reveals the honed Calacatta marble backsplash, stainless steel and solid walnut drawer fronts, and La Cornue stove.

PREVIOUS PAGES: An entire wall of the master bedroom is glass, providing treetop views and access to an upper terrace. The bed and the chaise—in the same deep charcoal as the living room sofa—offer views of the exterior and the bedroom fireplace.

RIGHT: For maximum enjoyment, a soaking tub sits in front of the large darkened steel window, which opens the master bath to the lush vistas. The marble sink with a deep front bib is set in a recess lined with warm walnut wood and Calacatta marble. A painting by Saba Jawda adds another graphic note.

ABOVE: In true Mediterranean style, the home is surrounded by dual courtyard walls, one vine-covered facing the street and the other a tumbled stone set in plaster. A wooden entrance gate gives the impression of a Mediterranean country house.

RIGHT: Seen as a whole, the Stolle residence combines modern forms with Mediterranean materials and ideas of indoor-to-outdoor flow and transparency. In addition to the lush lawn, private, personally focused gardens, terraces, and courtyards extend each of the rooms on the ground floor.

MEDITERRANEAN: EXPLORATIONS IN NOSTALGIA

In creating the romance of the Mediterranean—without a cliché arch or clay tile—I have been exploring the impact of natural materials and rounded/arched forms. In the concept design for a hotel in Houston, the use of half arches hearkens back to a regal, historic past. Precious relics in the form of echoes of arches, vaults, and black-and-white tile floors in the lobby are captured in their essence though contemporary in form and design. The illusion of Old World Mediterranean style also emerges in the reflection of the lobby's deep bronze glass and polished floor.

domus
Alvar Aalto
ARCHITECTURE
BEER

CRAFTS REVIVAL

In the late 1990s a style that could be called "New Antiquarian" began to emerge in the United States, as evidenced by the Soho Grand and ACE hotels. Numerous restaurants from Seattle to Manhattan began to create new environments that appeared as if they had been there, complete with decoration and accessories, since the late 1800s. Though I enjoy these environments, I do not take pleasure in copying the past; instead, I prefer to re-create the mood and foster nostalgia by using contemporary details and materials, juxtaposed with the kind of care and craft that existed before the Industrial Age. Thus I categorize this body of my work as Crafts Revival.

"Luxury Liberated," a term I learned from Brad Wilson, now president of ACE Hotel Group, might be the best way to describe my version of Crafts Revival. It also describes the Bloomsbury Group, whom I had studied in art history. They were a kind of social arts club and movement started by artist/designer Vanessa Bell and her sister, author Virginia Woolf, in the early 1900s in London. The Bloomsbury Group rejected bourgeois habits and lived a bohemian lifestyle, holding weekly social nights at their homes, where they discussed current philosophies. From philosopher G. E. Moore, for example, they adopted the notion that "one's prime objects in life were love, the creation and enjoyment of aesthetic experience, and the pursuit of knowledge." Not only was the Bloomsbury Group a precursor of the current "writing club" trend, but they were also advocates of the intrinsic value of things, which I feel drives the current passion for nostalgic and handcrafted design. In other words, the love of experience and the collection of memories is more greatly treasured than riches.

The details and care that go into individually handcrafted work embody the kind of luxury that is valued by those who can own any brand-name items they desire but often want something that is more intriguing or special. When people ask me what I think luxury is, I remember visiting Akumal, Mexico, twenty-five years ago, when it was just a pristine beach with tents set under the tall palm trees, and the menu was whatever the hotel's kitchen staff could catch that day or gather from the grounds. There's a purity to natural, handmade objects that have been created out of need yet designed to aesthetically please their owner. The desire for handcrafted pieces also involves a respect for local craftspeople and an appreciation of sustainable goods that are not mass-produced in environmentally damaging or unhealthy conditions.

In addition to the benefit to the environment, there are aesthetic benefits to using

earthy, handcrafted elements: they have made many Modern, Minimal, and Midcentury Modern designs more intriguing and iconic. For example, Albert Frey's Modernist Palm Springs house weaves an exterior rock outcropping into the interiors, and Wharton Esherick's Pennsylvania house features an organic hand-carved staircase.

A renaissance of craft can also be seen in today's furniture design, such as chairs by the Campana brothers and Patricia Urquiola's handcrafted products. My own furniture designs utilize solid woods, glass, and metals in an honest manner expressive of their natural states.

Good examples of Crafts Revival utilize raw textures and natural materials interwoven with contemporary and native traditions to make curious, elegant, and sophisticated environments, and I am intrigued to see that this move toward the natural and handcrafted is finding its way into office design as well. By embracing natural woods as though they are the new white, or by incorporating rugs patterned as if they are embroidered, we apply this new Crafts Revival aesthetic for any environment. This shift to tactile expressions of materials and furnishings brings unexpected awareness and pleasure wherever they appear.

LOCAL TEXTURE

FOUR SEASONS HOTEL BOGOTÁ

BOGOTÁ, COLOMBIA

Designing two Four Seasons hotels in the same city at once offered an exciting opportunity to create meaningful distinctions. Though only a few miles apart, the two hotels were quite different in their sites, clientele, and attitude. While the Four Seasons Casa Medina was situated in a traditional early 1940s brick building in more of a business district, the Four Seasons Bogotá property (formally the Charleston) was located in a 1980s building with little historically precious architecture in the Zona T—a burgeoning weekend destination with new stores and restaurants. The existing conditions of the latter included small individual buildings with low ceilings and four or fewer rooms per floor. The corridors were petite, yet each of the rooms possessed a lovely light-filled view onto an active street scene in front and onto the garden behind.

For the design, we took cues from the surrounding restaurants and local shops, which were made of indigenous wood with a handcrafted yet contemporary flair. In the Four Seasons Bogotá tale I invented for inspiration, my character was an artsy young fashion designer whose friends come to Bogotá to find the hidden treasures and enjoy the culinary delights. Assuming she entertained her guests at the property, we designed the hotel to accommodate their desires and habits, creating an intimate breakfast venue overlooking a lush courtyard by morning, a tiny bar for their personal use (open all day), and an outdoor cocktail patio for a nightcap overlooking the glamorous street scene.

Having discovered amazing beadwork in the fashion shops and woodwork and weavings at the local annual arts and crafts fair, we sought these materials as our tools for design. We reinterpreted the beadwork as a frieze above the banquette in the café and created the reception area, lobby, and living room out of woven wood. Since the ceilings were so low, we treated the guest rooms as boxes where we used the same material for the walls and ceilings as well as a mirror strategically placed to uplift and visually offset the low ceiling height. For the corridors, we created a custom wallpaper with some of the patterns we saw in the local crafts. Indigenous wood was used for doors, millwork, and furnishings. Local craftspeople were employed to make the hand-beaded drapery fabric, the cocktail tables, and the front desk.

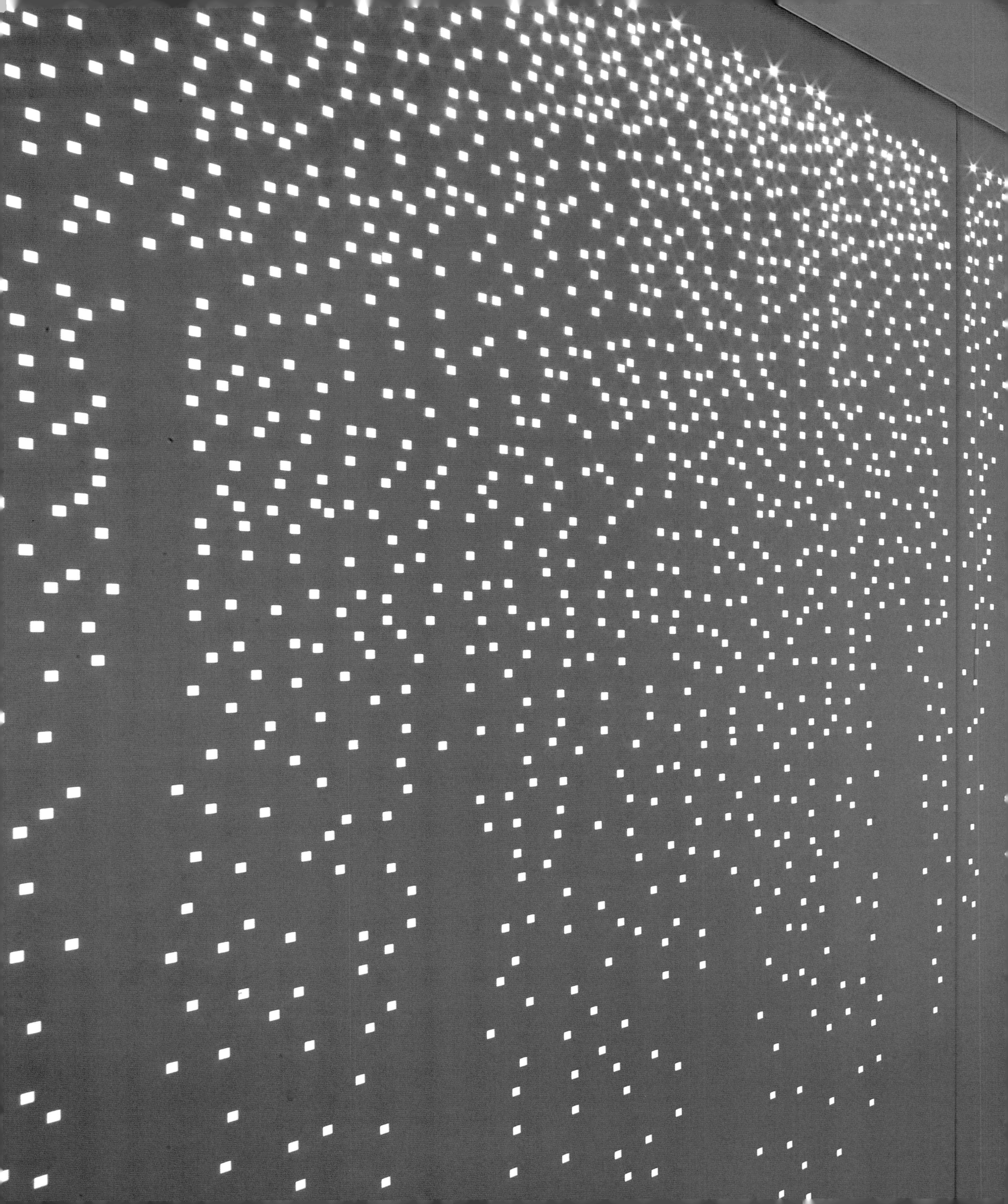

PREVIOUS PAGES: A locally sourced woven wood wall bends up onto the ceiling, engaging the guests as they linger in the hotel's living room, where sofas were upholstered deep emerald green as a nod to the Colombian rainforests. The Four Seasons meets Bogotá fashion district via a vine-covered arched trellis that flanks the entrance stairs to the hotel and emphasizes the lush greenery of the setting. A perforated metal wall evokes the calming effect of water droplets as the hallway leads to the spa treatment area.

ABOVE: Deep red leather-upholstered dining chairs complement the light warm leather banquettes and natural wood tables in the bar. A backdrop of locally sourced hand-beaded weavings in a colorful chevron pattern was chosen to identify the café as authentically Bogotá and authentically best-of-class in local fashion.

RIGHT: The guests' personal day and night bar is enhanced with elegant patterns of local wood joinery and marble marquetry.

Compared to the public spaces with their rich array of local colors and warm wood, the guest suites are more subdued, with pure white walls and modern, clean-lined furnishings, although rich, deep upholstery colors, lively pillow design, natural walnut, and hand-knotted drapery accent these spaces.

ANTIOQUIA
CASA DE CAMPO
COLOMBIA EN LE TOUR DU MONDE

WARMTH OF WOOD

MIDFIRST BANK MARKET STREET PRIVATE BANK

SCOTTSDALE, ARIZONA

With our design of its corporate offices in Scottsdale, Rottet Studio successfully created a brand and image for MidFirst Bank, an Oklahoma City–based institution, in the Arizona market. Their Market Street location in Scottsdale—Private Bank, as it has become known—serves as corporate offices for the President and CEO as well as a private branch location for major clients who require more personal service.

Compared to the rustic and traditional image of other MidFirst branch locations, Private Bank is much more contemporary in design and is intended to appeal to the specific clientele who frequent the location. MidFirst Private Bank incorporates the feeling of relaxed Arizona living with warm-colored natural Arizona stone and woods, and handcrafted, exposed wood beam construction. The clientele, when in Scottsdale, is typically there to relax at a second home or get away from the busy life of a major city, so we wanted to create an environment that would feel comfortable and reflect the calm desert when they needed to work instead of vacation. Every aspect of the space has been designed for enjoyment, including the vault, which features a natural wood table and leather chairs.

When I first began the project, I started with white as my background as I had always done before, then I realized that white was not appropriate as a background for a space that was meant to convey the natural warm tones of the desert. I told my team, "The natural color of walnut is the new white," and that we must transform our thinking to deal with this earthier background instead of our typical white drywall details. Floors were natural oak and beams raw steel and lumber. The client became so intrigued with the process of designing the space that he worked with me on the design of the main table and even created a little stick model of how the lumber legs, if stacked right, could support the top without additional structure.

The art selected to emphasize the respect for the natural desert attitude includes two Mie Olise paintings that hang in the second-floor "idea room" and a Chuck Close photograph of Kara Walker in the reception conference room.

PREVIOUS PAGES: A select group of branches is treated like poetry against the horizontal planks of natural walnut at the entrance to the MidFirst Bank Market Street, a private bank in Scottsdale, Arizona. In the vault lined with shiny steel security boxes in a regiment of sizes, a simple Bernhardt Design chair joins a wood table with extraordinary large tripod wood legs.

LEFT: Light and shade are themes throughout the bank. Accessed through a glass courtyard door, the reception area is deep in shadow. The patch artwork is by Ann Hamilton.

ABOVE: An artwork by Annette Schröter provides a backdrop for the reception desk made of walnut and dark bronze.

ABOVE: The walnut-paneled meeting room is simply appointed with a natural walnut conference table and credenza concealing refrigerated drawers. A photograph of Kara Walker by Chuck Close plays off an obsidian sculpture by William Cannings.

OPPOSITE, CLOCKWISE FROM ABOVE LEFT: Details of Crafts Revival include such items as a sawhorse-style desk with stainless steel legs, art books, highly textured rugs and upholstery fabrics, and bold gestural artworks as well as intricate pieces that elicit reflection.

LUXURY LIBERATED

THE JAMES
Royal Palm

THE JAMES ROYAL PALM

MIAMI, FLORIDA

When our team designed The James Royal Palm, we planned it as a tribute to the 1940s high life of Cuba and the late Art Deco roots of the original Royal Palm Hotel, which was built in 1939. The James Royal Palm, located on famous Collins Avenue, had been deemed a contributing representative of the Miami Beach Art Deco style, and therefore all design elements needed to be approved by Miami Beach's Historic Preservation Board. We also wanted to respect the hotel's history of notable guests, including Clark Gable and Franklin Delano Roosevelt Jr., as well as its significance as the first African American–owned hotel in South Beach.

While our design is partially the reincarnation of the historic Art Deco hotel, it is also contemporary—fresh and unpredictable, reflecting the James brand of "Luxury Liberated." We renovated the 179 guest rooms and 211 studios and suites, turning them into fanciful light-filled rooms with Deco colors and patterns and a strategically placed mirror to capture each room's ocean views. As well, we repositioned the two swimming pools, beachfront restaurant, poolside bar, and lobby lounge, and added a full-service spa.

Signature guest room elements include patterned wooden headboards that extend along the walls to work/dining niches featuring tables adorned with sunken blue glass tops. There are simple white lacquer bed stands and floral rugs patterned after one of my mother's embroidered footstools in shades of cerulean and sea blue. As an homage to the hotel's local legacy, our overall design preserved much of the original building's details and flourishes while fully embodying the James's warm, modern aesthetic. Simultaneously, we captured South Beach's extraordinary of-the-moment energy. Our vision was to transport guests into an era of nostalgia reminiscent of Art Deco Miami from the 1920s through the 1940s, an era that was all about being contemporary and progressive and living in the moment. Inspired by the Bloomsbury Group of bohemian creatives, I used Virginia Woolf coupled with Jean-Michel Basquiat as my characters for this hotel script. I imagined these two kindred souls from generations apart meeting while walking the beach and deciding to join each other for a few days of conversation and artistic philosophizing.

Several design elements pay particular homage to Miami's late Deco period, particularly the colors of muted green, orange, and tan; patterns and fabrics expressive of tropical Copacabana days; and a grand sweeping staircase on the hotel's first floor. Outside, on the property's rolling front lawn, we created a "moon gate," a topiary that frames the entrance and serves as a privacy screen for the garden. Furnished with oversized topiary chairs, the garden serves as an outdoor living room for guests and features the royal palm trees for which the hotel was named. Other signature design elements we kept that were original to the hotel include a decorative compass rose on the terrazzo lobby floor, porthole windows in the lounge, and the green glass reception desk, which we repurposed into the morning coffee and juice bar.

I was the official curator for the James Royal Palm's permanent art collection, entitled "An Ocean Apart," referring to the unique microculture found in Miami, which is the confluence of American, European, and Latin American cultures, unified by the lure of the ocean and iconic Miami Beach. The hotel's collection features local artists as well as nationally and internationally recognized art world luminaries. As an advocate of art and design education, I also incorporated several paintings from local art students. This once-in-a-lifetime exhibiting opportunity provides the youth with a positive outlet and encourages artistic growth within the community. The private collection of paintings, photographs, and prints led CNN to dub the hotel one of "7 artsy hotels around the world."

PREVIOUS PAGES: I designed the Collins Street signage for the James Royal Palm to immediately evoke a 1940s Miami Deco vibe and to introduce the guest to the restored Deco and contemporary handcrafted touches inside the hotel.

OPPOSITE: The lobby staircase is a cascade of wood-and-metal design also indicative of Crafts Revival. On the reinterpreted terrazzo floor rest two chairs with unique sidearm extensions reminiscent of the 1950s, with custom fabric inspired by surfboard art and upholstered by Lily Jack. The painting is by Patricia Schnall Gutierrez.

Morris Lapidus

The large porthole windows and the ship-like feeling of this lobby area were preserved in the hotel's redesign. The near wall features custom walnut panels, while a bold photograph by Alex Prager anchors the far wall. The furnishings have unique angles, and the hand-printed leather upholstery with art by Charles Arnoldi pays homage to the Florida Deco era. Light dances across the glossy terrazzo flooring here and throughout.

CAMPARI
APEROL
ST-GERMAIN
SOLERNO

A starburst clock has its own special niche in the feature wall of the restaurant bar, where boomerang shapes articulate the white shelving set against 45-degree-angled walnut paneling. In addition to the 1950s-style clock, the bar features other classic 1940s and '50s Jazz Age ceramics and an original James Hotel cabinet.

Drenched in green light, the bar area incorporates two Oculus pendant lights by Hot Glass Studio and a back-painted glass display case filled with green glassware and Deco collectibles. I began gathering green glass everywhere I went to fil the shelves before opening day.

LEFT & ABOVE, LEFT: In the reception lobby seating area, a collection of Cuban cigar boxes decorate a low glass duplex table of my design. Custom hand-printed Deco-style drapery frames the background view.

ABOVE, RIGHT: A Coalesse Shell Chair accompanies the dynamic, organically patterned custom area rug.

ABOVE: My team and I visited every room in the 400-room hotel to place furniture and mirrors to maximize the views. Playing on the ocean blue waters, I used a light-colored palette of blues, white, and natural oak to create a comfortable yet eclectic guest room.

OPPOSITE: Coastal Florida and its Miami Deco years provided many options and timeless modern inspirations for a Crafts Revival renovation of the James Royal Palm. An endless ocean view from one of the living room suites features a Meri side table from Oly Studio and a custom rug, both new interpretations of Crafts Revival.

Knoll Textiles

EXPRESSING THE BRAND

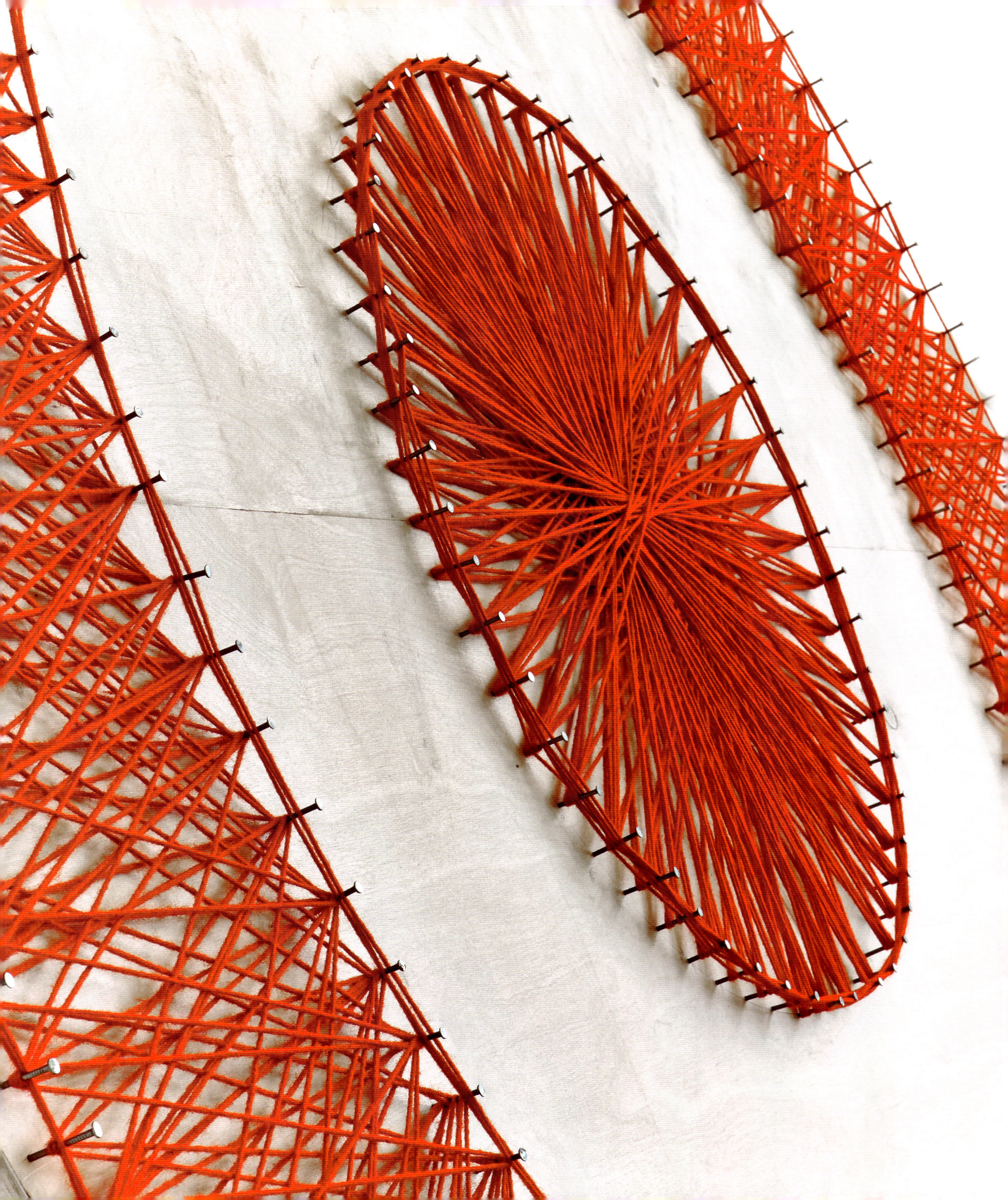

TARGET STUDIO

NEW YORK, NEW YORK

After searching for a long while, Target's chief creative officer, Todd Waterbury, and his team found the perfect venue in Chelsea for their marketing and creative offices. Accustomed to discerning good design from nonexistent, bad, or ordinary design, they appreciated our refined, quiet approach, and hired Rottet Studio to help them achieve their high goals for this important space.

As this location was also to serve as Target's public face for product launches, they wanted the environment to be more gallery- and loft-like than office-like. (Though Target's product is mass-produced to accommodate the volume they sell, they have an appreciation for items that are handcrafted from the heart and have a personal appeal.) To that end, within a warehouse-like building, Target took a ground-floor space visible from the street, similar to a Chelsea gallery, as well as a space on the second floor for their offices, product review, and display. For the upstairs functions, they sought a large, flexible space that could be opened up into one contiguous area during large product launches or closed off to create two separate but still sizable work spaces. For the design, Target desired a balance of raw loft-like natural space and precise, almost museum-like backdrops for clarity of purpose and display. Careful decisions were made about which of the "old loft" materials to keep—the thin plank wood floors, the exposed-wood-and-steel-beamed ceiling, and several existing brick walls made the cut—and what to cover and minimize. We also subtly incorporated the red "Target" marketing references to reinforce the brand without making it seem too overt.

Our approach accounted for tall ceilings, clean and durable finishes, and a design intended to serve as a background for product creation and product photography. Despite the loud red logo and barking company mascot, Target asked that the interior design be somewhat visually quiet in order not to influence or distract from creativity. The result is a combination of clean, contemporary lines juxtaposed with the Old World industrial building's exposed timbers and hardwood floors.

One focal point of the project is the guest space, where a colorful stained-wood decoratively patterned island offers lockers equipped with chargers and USB cables for visitors' personal belongings. Located adjacent to the kitchen, the island is the visual terminus at the end of the corridor between the two rooms, with large folding glass doors that open into one big entertainment space. The other focal point is the Target employee area. This private round conference/meeting room invites collaboration and exudes a homey feeling thanks to the surrounding built-in bookshelves. For the boardroom, we designed a red back-painted glass table to reflect the wallcovering custom-printed in bright red plaid, a pattern we designed for Target.

PREVIOUS PAGES: Offices for Target in a Chelsea warehouse loft capture the spirit of Crafts Revival, befitting Target's inclusive attitude to branding.

RIGHT: This classic Manhattan loft space has large windows, refinished rough wood floors, and the original radiators beneath the windows. The high ceilings allowed for the addition of a drop ceiling with illusive lighting. Accented by Target's logo made out of yarn, furnishings include a low-slung sofa and a low table on a custom rug as well as a Brancusi-style wood-block side table typical of Crafts Revival, which borrows from both museum art and pop art. The distinctive red brand color dots its way through a wall of Target imagery and artworks.

OPPOSITE: A recessed overhead lighting strip leads guests to a custom feature wall highlighting the locker area where they can store their personal belongings while visiting the space.

ABOVE: A painting from Target's collection gives the "Green Room" its name; here, classic modern furniture blends with new pieces to create a residential feel for the office.

ABOVE: The common area for Target's creative team features restrained hardwood floors with carpet tiles by Shaw. An acrylic chair by Vladimir Kagan dresses the room along with the Target mascot (and the occasional visiting dog).

OPPOSITE: A Target plaid was custom designed for covering the window spans and distracting attention from radiators, security window grilles, and exposed pipes. A table is set for communal eating with the Target creative staff.

CRAFTS REVIVAL: EXPLORATIONS IN HANDCRAFT

The predominance of handcrafted details in recent design is part of a larger reaction to—in some contemporary architecture—a lack of detail and soul. The concept design for a hotel in Washington, D.C., demonstrates how Rottet Studio and the Herzog & de Meuron design team embraced historical influence without mimicking it. The large third-floor lobby space was envisioned like an early American village where the inhabitants walk through the central atrium court from restaurant to bar to meeting halls. As in most colonial towns, the tavern restaurants are clad in wood, and the town hall is clad in stone, a return to the honesty of regional materials that is further evidenced in the natural walnut walls and leather-finished white marble tables. Walnut, bronze, limestone, and Calacatta marble forms sit inside the minimal metal and glass perimeter like sets waiting to be discovered.

Nusakan
Nekkar
Alkaid
Seginus
M51
Whirlpool
Galaxy
Izar
Arcturus
Muphrid
Vindemiatrix

THEATRICAL

The line between real life and theater life seems to shift in the contemporary world, where everyone has his or her fifteen minutes of fame, just as Andy Warhol predicted. While a theater provides a platform for dramatic action, a Theatrical design may provide a stage in which to live, work, or vacation. I think of Theatrical design as a dramatic presence for living, so "Theatrical" may mean design done in a way that is meant to attract attention or create a sense of drama—or maybe just to invite acute perception or expectation on the part of those entering a space or a room.

Theatrical design cannot go unnoticed and intentionally causes the occupant to pause, look around, and refocus his or her thoughts. Much as the start of a movie causes the theater to quieten while all focus turns to the screen, well-thought-out Theatrical design encourages the inhabitant to concentrate on the task at hand. Whether it is a question of focusing attention for a business meeting in an office environment or focusing attention on relaxing in a vacation environment, this style of design directs the individual through the space. In a Theatrical setting, the entry sets the tone, then the design intentionally lets the eye rest with moments of visual quiet giving way to moments of visual intensity, like a musical score leading up to a crescendo. The crescendo could be the boardroom or the bar or the penthouse suite, but in all cases of Theatrical design, the path leading to it prepares the occupant for the ultimate experience.

By way of a concrete example, I typically use orthogonal planes and symmetrical spaces for the entry, as it tends to calm and orient the senses. In some of our more theatrically based work, however, we use dramatic geometry to grab attention and focus the eye toward the next space in the sequence.

Another aspect of theatrically based design that I like to use in all of our projects is the element of surprise. My colleagues tell me that just when they think they know exactly what I will do with the design, I surprise them. The surprise must always be carefully done so as not to disrupt the overall feel of the environment, but including the unexpected is a wonderful way to keep the user engaged with the space and counteract any boredom or complacency. For example, a dramatic wall mural presides over the stair at United Talent Agency in Beverly Hills. I often use art as the element of surprise, or I employ a dramatic pattern or color inside a drawer or closet. Then there are the real theaters that we have created, such as the screening room at United Talent Agency in Los Angeles, where my partner Richard Riveire created high drama in golden wood tones with what we might call a rhetorical display of terraced, plush-seated applause.

Incorporating theatrical moves into our design heightens the experience for the occupants and their visitors. The result also allows us to enjoy the real-life movies we at Rottet Studio have helped create by setting the stage. Drama may reign, but still, the design choices are never gratuitous. These are not just stages for show—they are stages for living and working. As such, it's important to us that all of the choices are authentic to the needs of the occupants and to the way the space will be used. This is how to bestow even the most theatrical spaces with a timeless appeal.

We might even call these designs truly "special" because with this attitude, we can turn a mundane parking garage, as at United Talent Agency in Los Angeles, into a dynamic, engaging entrance hall. Or we can treat structural walls in an office like Paul Hastings LLP in Chicago as sculptural pieces reminiscent of the city's historic architecture—which share a kinship to monumental Richard Serra sculptures. A Viking ocean liner can have a Winter Garden that visually transports viewers to an environment with manmade "trees." It is the drama of dynamic design statements leading to a crescendo that sets these designs apart.

DYNAMIC PRESENCE

PAUL HASTINGS LLP

CHICAGO, ILLINOIS

We chose a Theatrical approach for international law firm Paul Hastings's Chicago office because it offered a dynamic client and visitor experience that captured city views from all sides of the uniquely shaped building. Chicago's rich art and architecture history inspired our design concept, which echoed shapes and forms found in the city's skyscraper window vernacular and in many of the city's iconic sculptures. The design of the rug inset within the reception and conference center is a visual metaphor for the city's river, which runs through downtown; its ripples radiate from the inner core of the reception area outward toward the view. In an abstract manner, it also captures Chicago's amazing skyline and surrounding Great Lakes.

The area where the attorneys practice is sequestered from the conference center, with administrative support staff strategically clustered at the east and west arcs of the elliptical-shaped building. Centralizing support staff helps to maximize team interaction and foster a more collaborative, efficient workplace. We removed an existing wall that defined the private offices along the building's perimeter and replaced it with a glass storefront system. The new glazing wall was installed two feet inside of where the old wall stood in order to reduce the excess "dead space" within each private office and to give more square footage to the common area corridor. The result was more of an open-office environment, where natural sunlight can pierce deeper into the core of the building.

The new Chicago space reflects Paul Hastings's creative and forward-thinking philosophy and its image as a leading international law firm. The environment also supports the firm's goals of enabling its teams to work smarter and more collaboratively.

PREVIOUS PAGES: In a city renowned for its architecture, the Chicago offices of Paul Hastings were devised as a theatrical play on structure. Large wood shapes animate the reception area and allow background light to filter in, causing guests to question what is wall and what is ceiling.

LEFT: Areas along the perimeters were opened to the continuous view of the city, and a Tai Ping carpet was selected in a style that serves as a metaphor for the Chicago River. It also unifies the various areas of low, unobtrusive seating. On the interior core wall at right, the wood box shapes—defined by light—continue into the open-seating office space.

ABOVE: A close view of the inset chandelier, designed by me and rendered by 3form, reveals its faceted acrylic parts and rich gilded background.

AUDIENCE ENGAGEMENT

UNITED TALENT AGENCY

BEVERLY HILLS, CALIFORNIA

Theatrical is an appropriate style for industries that reflect the latest in culture, especially the entertainment industry. When United Talent Agency (UTA) commissioned us to design their new headquarters in Beverly Hills, we knew a Theatrical design would be the right fit for one of the premier talent agencies in the business.

UTA wanted their new facility to reflect their success and permanence in the industry while also providing a comfortable and collaborative environment for their staff and clients. Since UTA is a client-driven organization and in the entertaining business, our design team sought to create a powerful first impression while ensuring a comfortable guest experience.

As one might expect, a talent agency is in the business of attracting the best talent to be their clients and then securing for them the best parts from the best production teams in the industry. Making the right impression with this "A" team from the entry throughout the rest of the space is critical; we knew the talent should feel protected and, above all, special. The building was set far back from the street, which made drop-offs at the front door difficult. With all challenges come opportunities, however, and we realized that we could cut an opening from the street-level lobby into the garage below. Los Angeles is a driving city, and the car matters—as does the garage—so we embraced this fact and created an environment where the talent literally almost drives right in. Once they're inside, the theatrical experience begins with a dramatic five-story stair leading from the garage entry up into the agency floors. Inside the lobby, guests are greeted by a highly customized reception desk designed to be slightly low so as to engage, not intimidate, the visitor. Next to it is a custom-designed angular sofa where a number of guests can sit at one time without feeling lined up in a row. Behind the reception area are private restrooms with excellent lighting so guests may freshen up before their meeting.

UTA's impressive art collection, selected by CEO Jeremy Zimmer, was a driving force in the design and in the theatrical experience. Though the collection consists mainly of large-scale fine art photography, Jeremy chose an impressive huge sculpture of the word "NO" to greet visitors at the base of the stair in our newly designed garage lobby entry. Serving as an element of surprise, this sets the tone for the rest of the art, with plenty of conversation pieces to break the ice and

relieve any tensions. Our project team designed the space not only to accommodate the required functions but also to serve as a gallery. Several large pieces were specifically commissioned for the project as well, including a large tapestry by Pae White and a light sculpture by John Wigmore.

A screening room was of utmost importance as UTA frequently has clients—including A-list celebrities—join them for private screenings. Our design team created a 165-seat theater from part of the existing parking garage, enclosed it with cement walls, and outfitted it with unparalleled acoustic and projection equipment. State-of-the art technology allows for the screening of Hollywood's latest blockbuster movies, television episodes, independent films, and video games, as well as for lectures and meetings. It was not long before the *Los Angeles Times* praised the space, noting that, "For an agency, it's probably the best screening room that exists."

Although UTA did not specify a need for LEED certification, their partners wanted the project to incorporate as many aspects of sustainable/green design as possible. Nearly all of the materials chosen for the project were low in volatile organic compounds (low VOC) to reduce toxic air quality. The lighting for the project is almost entirely composed of LED systems to reduce energy costs. Large glass walls were incorporated into the design of internal offices to maximize the amount of natural light and thereby reduce the need for electricity during the day. We were also able to reuse some of the existing furniture, and where we could not, we used as many local materials and manufacturers as possible to reduce the carbon footprint associated with transportation costs. In keeping with contemporary design standards, we also incorporated multiple terraces to allow employees and guests a variety of work and meeting environments.

PREVIOUS PAGES: In a city of entertainment, the United Talent Agency was an ideal client for a design with theatrical allusions, as seen in the screening room, reception area, and parking entrance area. Large sculptures in the parking reception area by John Miller titled *Portable Negotiation* accompany a painting in the seating area titled *El Vino De Espiritu* by RETNA.

RIGHT: In the office of CEO Jeremy Zimmer, comfortable seating with a low marble table offers an environment for unintimidating conversation and an opportunity to enjoy artwork by Miriam Svet Schary, Jeremy's mother (left), and Edward Ruscha (right).

RICHTER
TO CAGE DOMINIC DAVIES
JOEL STERNFELD SWEET EARTH

FLOATING STAGE

VIKING STAR

VIKING CRUISE SHIP

Our relationship with Viking Cruises started as a dream of designing amazingly beautiful contemporary ships based on architectural thought rather than overpowering decoration. I had renovated a yacht for a close friend and client, and I quickly discovered the world of ship design and the speed and agility with which the crews could change out interiors while at port. I fell in love with the allure of this world and decided to pursue it further.

It seemed like the dream had been realized when the following week a call came in about the possibility of designing for Viking River Cruises. My partner Richard Riveire's charm and deep talent won them over, and we have now completed well over forty river cruise ships and three ocean ships. We continue to design for Viking, creating theatrical yet calm and architectural environments never before seen in the cruise industry—captivating, fresh, open, contemporary spaces that inspire and intrigue, providing stimulation and comfort no matter how long the cruise.

One project of particular note was the design of the *Viking Star*, the line's first foray into ocean cruising, in 2015. As Torstein Hagen, chairman of Viking Cruises, noted, "With the launch of our ocean division, we have created a new kind of vessel—smaller in size and smarter in design—an alternative to today's mega-liners."

Richard engaged in every nuance of the Viking experience. When he and Torstein looked at the structure of the steel dome covering the *Viking Star*'s glass retractable roof, they were struck by its similarities to the great nineteenth-century greenhouses. This observation led to the idea of a Winter Garden: a place for guests to relax in the sun while enjoying a cup of tea. The real fun, Richard noted, came when they introduced the imagery of the Norse god Odin's exploring ravens. They created wood lattice-work tree-like structures for the mythological ravens Huginn and Muninn to enjoy. In a decidedly theatrical way, the shadows cast by the steel and wood make lovely patterns, as in a forest with dappled sunlight.

Every part of the *Viking Star* was designed to maximize guests' destination experience and keep them entertained throughout the cruise in good or bad weather. Viking wanted the pool to serve as a setting for exploration. The designers created one of the first oceangoing infinity pools, so guests feel like they are in the heart of their destination, relaxing in a glass-backed pool cantilevered off the ship's stern. In the evening, the pool deck transforms into the Aquavit Terrace, where there is alfresco dining while the world floats by.

The *Viking Star* living room is rich in nautical nuances—the rugs are stylized versions of architectural drawings of ancient Viking ships, with elevations, cross sections, and plans all represented in various scales, and macramé window dressings are reminiscent of traditional Norwegian handiwork. The ribbed forms in the ceiling, the integrated metalwork, and the use of wood paneling were also inspired by original Viking ships. In particular, the living room's wooden bar is an example of true Viking craftsmanship—clinker-built, just as the original Viking longships were constructed, with overlapping panels of smooth wood.

Viking Star's Penthouse Junior Suites and Explorer Suites feature large private verandas providing natural light and sweeping views. These suites reflect Scandinavian design influences in the use of streamlined furnishings, abundant wood, neutral tones, and natural fabrics in beiges, creams, ocean blues, and soft grays.

PREVIOUS PAGES: Water on water is the striking appearance of *Viking Star*'s infinity pool, allowing guests to immerse themselves in views of the vast sky and endless ocean horizons. Viking Star is the first of many oceangoing vessels in the Viking fleet. All aspects of the ship were thought out from a design perspective to give the traveler an unparalleled experience.

RIGHT: A glazed staircase floats through the glass-roofed and glass-walled solarium of the Discovery Lounge at the bow of the vessel. The curved shape of the divisionary line between the interior wood flooring and the carpet emulates the ship's hull as it glides effortlessly through the sea.

PREVIOUS PAGES: Theatrical aptly describes the feeling of *Viking Star*'s Winter Garden with wood lattice tree-like structures that form the double-height space and emphasize the retractable roof. The bar anchors the center, and casual seating groupings welcome guests throughout. Side scenes include cutout landscape forms in the corners, and even a silhouette reference to the mythological Norse ravens, at right on the lintel.

OPPOSITE: At the stair landing in the three-story grand hall, an ever-changing high-definition screen showcases landscapes from Viking's travels.

THIS PAGE, CLOCKWISE FROM ABOVE, LEFT: Woven macramé window coverings evoke a handmade Nordic craft quality and precise attention to detail in the living room. A custom-carved hardwood console houses the restaurant's concierge desk. Past the glazed steel and glass minimal staircase are views looking forward of the *Viking Star*'s bow.

THEATRICAL:
EXPLORATIONS IN STAGECRAFT

The guest's search for the ultimate experience has led me to think beyond physical surroundings to create an immersive story in which fantasy and discovery prevail. The concept design for a hotel in Mexico City (right and opposite, above) conjures a world based on the alluring mythology of a city floating over crystal-filled waters and on the influences of Mayan astrology. A dramatic lobby stair weaves its way up to the restaurants, creating a grand chandelier effect with cut-crystal patterns reflected on the ceiling and floor, and the lights in the ceiling are reminiscent of Mayan constellations. A fire pit created out of vapor and video and a circular glass surround with tree patterns represent "a walk to the woods." The design for the indoor pool of a luxury high-rise in Manhattan (opposite, below) hearkens back to the theatrical glamour of Hearst Castle.

ACKNOWLEDGMENTS

This book would not have happened without the wonderful work of my friend Elizabeth McMillian, of Kyle Rottet, and of Ruthie Chen, who pushed this book through with what seems to be apparent ease. And Melody Faircloth, who works miracles behind the scenes. I would also like to thank Aliza Fogelson and the team at Rizzoli New York for their patience and expertise in helping this book come to life.

In addition to my personal family, I wish to thank my principal partners Richard Riveire, David Davis, and Jeff Records.

From the first day I worked with Richard Riveire, I realized he was the ultimate Boy Scout: always prepared with a wealth of architectural and design knowledge from intense study and a healthy bag of tricks with which to accomplish any task. Together we have completed over fifty million square feet of built space, and his design talent, technical expertise, and dedication continue to guide our work.

David Davis came into our lives through mutual friends and brought with him the gifts of intuition, insight, and years of management experience, for which we are grateful. A wonderful designer in his own right, he expertly guides us to achieve outstanding work, balancing the many parts that compose the projects and the firm.

Jeff Records provided invaluable support for the launching of Rottet Studio and continues to guide and assist us with the business side of our practice.

I extend my deepest appreciation to the Rottet Studio family, who have been the most supportive and creative of any in the industry:

Our leadership: Harout Dedeyan, Donna Gutierrez, Josef Jelinek, Stuart Laff, Anja Majkic, Patricia McCaul, and Enrique Vela. Our design and technical leaders: Michael Au, Mark Borkowski, Laurence Cartledge, James Cull, Chris Evans, Jeff Horning, Chris Jones, Jin Lee, Amber Lewis, Jennifer Mateo, Bernardo Rios, Winnie Wong, and our amazing team: Kristin Amundsen, Kaitlin Borgen, Ruthie Chen, Hokulea Duffett, Melody Faircloth, Lori Firpo, Taylor Fleck, Clara Goitia, Jeremiah Hahn, Ginny Hightower, Maksim Koloskov, Theresa Lee, Ashley Liu, Wade Meadors, Ana Maria Nater, Edgar Rivera, Samantha Roberts, Jaime Roveri, Kyle Rottet, Angel Sanchez, Zina Sharif, April Smith, Brooke Walker, and Jessica Yong. I also want to thank Ndemina Abbiyesuku, Leyla Aghayeva, Kai Broms, Tammy Chan, Nicholas Coker, Doug Cottle, Alana Davidson, Erin Dorey, Kevin Engellenner, Daniel Epperson, Simona Furini, Brian Gabbard, Sona Gevorkyan, Adam Gibson, Caitlin Graham, Corey Greer, Arlene Hacatoryan, Marissa Iacovoni, Toheed Khawaja, Gregorz Kosmal, Armand Kostanian, Ben Koush, Christy Landrum, Charles Lee,

Kefan Lu, Carrie Lust, Michelle Manuel, Michelle Mulitz, Angelique Nossa, Chris Olexy, Kayla Rodd, Ashleigh Rogers, DeeDee Sanchez, Michelle Sterling, Emmy Thammasine, Ben Verceles, Ronda Wang, Eric Wattanachote, Jodi White, and Rose Wilkowski. And the team while with DMJMRottet: Naomi Asai, Tina Fajardo, Leslie Grant, Andrea Handel, Vano Haritunians, Alice Hricak, Luci Iwasaki, Michael Montanez, and Joey Shimoda.

I particularly want to thank our clients, who graciously allowed me to design and then publish their projects. Without their invaluable trust and support over the years, my visions would never exist, including and in addition to those whose projects are covered in the book:

Michael Allen, Anadarko Petroleum Corporation, Andell Holdings, Annenberg Foundation, Arel Capital, Artis Capital Management, Barbara Davis Gallery, Gary Barnett, Brooke Barrett, Alex and Ann Bernhardt, Bernhardt Design, BGI Group, Lloyd Blankfein, BMC Investments, Daniel Boulud, Donald Brin, Caesars Entertainment, Capital Group American Funds, Carpenter & Company, Inc., Cisterra Development, Comcast, CommonWealth Partners, Crescent Real Estate Properties, Mike Croft and Lynn Williams, Jeff Dash, Patrick Denihan, Denihan Hospitality Group, The Dinex Group, Dorchester Collection, Duff & Phelps, Extell Development Company, Tom Farley, Foley & Lardner LLP, Four Seasons Hotels and Resorts, Bill and Melinda Gates, GEM Realty, Molly Gochman, Goldman Sachs, GPI Companies, Doyle Graham, Grove Street Partners, Torstein and Karine Hagen, Andrew and Ellen Hauptman, Haynes and Boone LLP, Jerry Helling, Hidrock Properties, Hilton Hotels and Resorts, Hines, Houston Center, The Hudson Partnership, Hyatt Hotels Corporation, The Irvine Company, Scott Johnson, Johnson Downie, Johnson Fain, Dana Kalczak, Katia Boutique, Bonnie Kelley, Mahmood and Naznin Khimji, Kimpton Hotel and Restaurant Group, Kirkland & Ellis LLP, Langham Hospitality Group, Liberty Property Trust, Richard Liebovitch, Dr. K.S. Lo, Katherine Lo, Loews Hotels & Resorts, Howard Marks, Marriott International, Mattel, McKinsey & Company, MidFirst Bank, Midway Companies, Montage Hotels & Resorts, Brandi Montgomery, Morgans Hotel Group, Morrison Foerster, Miki Naftali, Naftali Group, New York Stock Exchange, Nixon Peabody LLP, Northwestern Mutual, Oaktree Capital Management, Pacific Eagle, Palisades Capital Partners, Patrinely Group, Paul Hastings LLP, Pendry Hotels, PennyMac, Lisa Perrine, Stuart Peterson, Pontiac Land Group, Pat Ramsey, Jeff Records, Red Mountain Capital Partners, The Redstone Companies, Regent Partners, Rising Realty Partners, Ritz-Carlton Hotel Company, Dr. Ramin M. Roohipour, Sedesco, Dr. Jennifer Segal, Sentinel Trust Company, Seyfarth Shaw LLP, Izzy Sharp, Shell Oil Company, Skadden, Arps, Slate, Meagher & Flom LLP, Sony Music Entertainment, Snell & Wilmer LLP, Jeffrey Sprecher, Starwood Hotels and Resorts, Kevin Stolle, St. Regis Hotels & Resorts, Target Corporation, Jon Tisch, Tootsies, Trafigura, United Talent Agency, Valencia Group, Viacom, Viking Cruises, Vinson & Elkins LLP, Dr. Paul Vitenas, The Walt Disney Company, Wanxiang Group, Todd Waterbury, Wells Fargo Plaza, Wheelock Properties, Stacy Wilder, Brad Wilson, Debbie Wilson, Seth Zachary, Zadok Jewelers, and Jeremy Zimmer.

CREDITS

Page 1: See Contemporary Grandeur/ Private Residence (below)

Page 2: Conrad Hotel at CityCenterDC, Washington, D.C.
Project Team: Lauren Rottet, David Davis, Anja Majkic, Enrique Vela, Bernardo Rios, Kristin Amundsen, Kaitlin Borgen, Jessica Yong, Alana Davidson, Carolina Castarella, Marquez Colby
Renderer: Enrique Vela, Leyla Aghayeva

Page 4: See Mediterranean Redefined/Stolle Residence (opposite)

Page 10: New Hotel Concept, Mexico City, Mexico
Project Team: Lauren Rottet, David Davis, Kelie Mayfield, Anja Majkic, Bernardo Rios, Chris Evans, Brian Gabbard, Christopher Olexy, DeeDee Sanchez, Carrie Lust
Renderer: Tom Rusteberg

Page 13: See Mediterranean Redefined/Stolle Residence (opposite)

Page 15: Barbara Davis Gallery, Houston, Texas
Project Team: Lauren Rottet, Anja Majkic, Ben Koush
Artist: Andrea Bianconi
Photographer: Jeremy Keas

Page 16: See Visual Movement/Rottet Residence (below)

Page 19: Haynes & Boone, LLP, Houston, Texas
Project Team: Lauren Rottet, Anja Majkic, Todd Runkle, Erick Ragni, Bernardo Rios, Tuan Nguyen, Christy Landrum
Photographer: FOTOWORKS (Benny Chan)

Page 20: AECOM Technology Corporation, New York, New York
Project Team: Lauren Rottet, Naomi Asai, Vano Haritunians, Alice Hricak, Ramesh Laridjani
Photographer: Michael Moran

MODERN

Paul Hastings LLP, Los Angeles (page 26)
Project Team: Lauren Rottet, Richard Riveire, Naomi Asai, Michael Au, Vano Haritunians, Alice Hricak, Jefferson Choi
Photographer: Hedrich Blessing (Nick Merrick)

Seamless Integration/Paul Hastings LLP, Frankfurt, Germany (pages 28–33)
Project Team: Lauren Rottet, Kelie Mayfield, Ben Koush, Alice Hricak, Laine Gregory, Simona Furini, Laurence Cartledge
Photographer: Eric Laignel

Transparency/Artis Capital Management, San Francisco, California (pages 34–45)
Project Team: Lauren Rottet, Kelie Mayfield, Kai Broms, Michael Au, Sandy Lam, Christopher Olexy, Laine Gregory, Tom Rusteberg, Maksim Koloskov
Photographer: Eric Laignel

Visual Movement/Rottet Residence, Montauk, New York (pages 16, 46–59)
Project Team: Lauren Rottet, Jane O'Brien
Photographers: Scott Frances (pages 48, 52, 53, 56, 57, 58–59), Emily Gilbert (pages 16, 46, 51, 54, 55)

Refined Order/Financial Management Firm, New York, New York (pages 60–69)
Project Team: Lauren Rottet, David Davis, Enrique Vela, DeeDee Sanchez, Chris Evans, Mark Borkowski
Photographer: Eric Laignel

Reflectivity & Illusion/Paul Hastings LLP, New York, New York (pages 22–23, 70–77)
Project Team: Lauren Rottet, Todd Runkle, Grzegorz Kosmal, Naomi Asai, Michael Au, Tammy Chan, Alice Hricak, Michelle Manuel
Photographer: Michael Moran

Loews Houston, Houston, Texas (pages 78–79 [right and opposite, above])
Project Team: Lauren Rottet, Anja Majkic, Kristin Amundsen, Maksim Koloskov
Renderer: Tim Bogza

The River Oaks Condominiums, Houston, Texas (page 79 [opposite, below])
Project Team: Lauren Rottet, Anja Majkic, Amber Lewis, Jessica Yong
Renderer: Tim Bogza

MINIMAL

Captivating Quiet/Bernhardt Design Showroom, New York, New York (pages 80–81, 86–95)
Project Team: Lauren Rottet, David Davis, Josef Jelinek, James Cull, Ashley Liu, Kefan Lu
Photographer: Eric Laignel

Rottet Studio, Los Angeles, California (pages 85 [right], 336)
Project Team: Lauren Rottet, Richard Riveire, Patricia McCaul, Harout Dedeyan, Charles Lee, Laurence Cartledge, Mark Borkowski, Jennifer Mateo, Winnie Wong, Jeremiah Hahn
Photographer: Arden Ash

Raw Beauty/Gochman Residence, Houston, Texas (pages 96–105)
Project Team: Lauren Rottet, Erick Ragni, Chris Evans, DeeDee Sanchez, Brian Gabbard
Photographer: Maksim Koloskov

Tranquil Illumination/Bernhardt Design Showroom, Chicago, Illinois (pages 85 [left], 106–115)
Project Team: Lauren Rottet, Kelie Mayfield, Chris Evans, Jeff Horning, Laurence Cartledge, Tom Rusteberg
Photographer: Eric Laignel

Langham Place Brand Development, Hong Kong, China (pages 116–117 [right])
Project Team: Lauren Rottet, Richard Riveire, David Davis, Enrique Vela, Harout Dedeyan, Charles Lee, Leyla Aghayeva, Ndemina Abbiyesuku, Kevin Engellenner, Kaitlin Borgen, Brooke Walker
Renderers: Enrique Vela, Transparent House, Joey Fonacier, Acusourcing

Mori Residential Tower, Yokohama, Japan (page 117 [opposite, above and below])
Project Team: Lauren Rottet, Kelie Mayfield, Chris Evans, Bernardo Rios, Maksim Koloskov, Christopher Olexy, Tom Rusteberg
Renderer: Tom Rusteberg

BEAUX-ARTS

Contemporary Grandeur/Private Residence, New York, New York (pages 118–119, 124–135)
Project Team: Lauren Rottet, David Davis, Christopher Olexy, Kaitlin Borgen, Kylie Sarley, Lori Firpo, Matthew Baird Architects
Photographer: Scott Frances

Classic Reinterpreted/Loews Regency Hotel, New York, New York (pages 122 [right], 136–141)
Project Team: Lauren Rottet, David Davis, Enrique Vela, Anja Majkic, DeeDee Sanchez, Kevin Engellenner, Bernardo Rios, Ndemina Abbiyesuku, Iris Etgar, Heather O'Donnell, Lori Firpo
Photographer: Michael Kleinberg

Haussmann's Paris Reflected/Paul Hastings LLP, Paris, France (pages 122 [left], 142–149)
Project Team: Lauren Rottet, Naomi Asai, Laurence Cartledge, Alice Hricak, Vano Haritunians
Photographer: Jimmy Cohrssen

Mountain Manor/The St. Regis Aspen Resort, Aspen, Colorado (pages 150–163)
Project Team: Lauren Rottet, David Davis, Simona Furini, Ashleigh Rogers, Christopher Olexy, Brian Gabbard, Carrie Lust, Alberto Govela
Photographer: Eric Laignel

Honoring Coco/The Surrey Hotel, New York, New York (pages 164–183)
Project Team: Lauren Rottet, David Davis, Richard Riveire, Kelie Mayfield, Chris Evans, Christopher Olexy, Laurence Cartledge, Mark Borkowski, Kristin Stang, Michelle Manuel, Tammy Chan, Heeyoung Lee, Grzegorz Kosmal, Emmy Thammasine, Armand Kostanian, DeeDee Sanchez, Ami Helmstetter, Lisa Ra, Lauren Weintraub, Carrie Lust
Photographers: Eric Laignel (164, 166, 169, 170, 172, 173, 174, 175, 177, 178, 179, 182, 183), Tom McWilliam (176, 180, 181)

Loews Regency, San Francisco, California (page 185 [right, above and below])
Project Team: Lauren Rottet, David Davis, Enrique Vela, Anja Majkic, James Cull, Ashley Liu, Kristin Amundsen, Mimi Li, Neha Sadruddin
Renderers: Ashley Liu, Tim Bogza, Leyla Aghayeva

Langham Brand Development, Hong Kong, China (page 184 [above])
Project Team: Lauren Rottet, Richard Riveire, David Davis, Enrique Vela, Harout Dedeyan, Charles Lee, Leyla Aghayeva, Ndemina Abbiyesuku, Kevin Engel enner, Kaitlin Borgen, Brooke Walker
Renderers: Enrique Vela, Transparent House, Joey Fonacier, Acusourcing

MEDITERRANEAN

Luxurious Bungalow/The Beverly Hills Hotel Presidential Bungalows, Beverly Hills, California (pages 191 [right], 192–201)
Project Team: Lauren Rottet, Richard Riveire, Harout Dedeyan, Laurence Cartledge, Mark Borkowski, Christopher Olexy, Heeyoung Lee, Winnie Wong
Photographer: Eric Laignel (191 [right], 192, 194, 197, 198, 199, 201), Fred Licht (200)

Romantic Colonial/Four Seasons Casa Medina, Bogotá, Colombia (page 191 [left], 202–213)
Project Team: Lauren Rottet, David Davis, Chris Evans, Amber Lewis, Ginny Hightower, Saul Sasson, Milena Vargas
Photographer: Molly Culver

Southern California Living, Croft Residence, Santa Monica, California (pages 214–225)
Project Team: Lauren Rottet, Charles Lee, Laurence Cartledge, Mark Borkowski, Winnie Wong, Bernardo Rios, Catherine Bailly Dunne, Bill McGregor
Photographer: FOTOWORKS (Benny Chan)

Mediterranean Redefined/Stolle Residence, Houston, Texas (pages 186–187, 226–245)
Project Team: Lauren Rottet, Anja Majkic, Erick Ragni, Chris Evans, Marissa Iacovoni, DeeDee Sanchez, Mia Jones
Photographer: Eric Laignel

Hotel Alessandra, Houston, Texas (pages 246–247)
Project Team: Lauren Rottet, Anja Majkic, Chris Evans, Jeff Horning, Kristin Amundsen, Maksim Koloskov, Erin Dorey, Jessica Yong
Renderer: Acusourcing

CRAFTS REVIVAL

10 Park Avenue Apartment, New York, New York (pages 248–249, 252)
Project Team: Lauren Rottet, David Davis, Brad Wilson, Rose Wilkowski, Adam Ruffin
Photographer: Ayla Christman

Local Texture/Four Seasons Hotel Bogotá, Bogotá, Colombia (pages 254–263)
Project Team: Lauren Rottet, Chris Evans, Amber Lewis, Ginny Hightower, Bernardo Rios, Marissa Iacovoni, Jessica Yong, Toheed Khawaja, Saul Sasson, Milena Vargas
Photographers: Eric Laignel (254, 256, 258–259, 260, 262–263), Molly Culver (261)

Warmth of Wood/MidFirst Bank Market Street Private Bank, Scottsdale, Arizona (pages 264–271)
Project Team: Lauren Rottet, Kelie Mayfield, Bernardo Rios, Jeff Horning, Jenny Chalfant, Angelique Nossa, Brian Gabbard, Kaitlin Borgen
Photographer: Eric Laignel

Luxury Liberated/The James Royal Palm, Miami Beach, Florida (pages 272–287)
Project Team: Lauren Rottet, David Davis, Anja Majkic, Enrique Vela, Bernardo Rios, Chris Evans, Carrie Lust, Kaitlin Borgen
Photographer: Eric Laignel

Expressing the Brand/Target Studio, New York, New York (pages 288–297)
Project Team: Lauren Rottet, David Davis, Enrique Vela, Josef Jelinek, Rose Wilkowski, Alana Davidson, Ashley Liu
Photographer: Eric Laignel

Conrad Hotel at CityCenterDC, Washington, D.C. (pages 298–299; see page 2 credits, opposite)

THEATRICAL

Dynamic Presence/Paul Hastings LLP, Chicago, Illinois (pages 306–311)
Project Team: Lauren Rottet, Richard Riveire, Harout Dedeyan, Yvonne Colacion, Charles Lee, Laurence Cartledge, Gabriel Huerta, Eric Wattanachote
Photographer: Hedrich Blessing (Steve Hall)

Audience Engagement/United Talent Agency, Beverly Hills, California (pages 305 [left], 312–319)
Project Team: Richard Riveire, Lauren Rottet, Patricia McCaul, Harout Dedeyan, Michelle Mulitz, Jennifer Mateo, Christopher Jones, Winnie Wong, Jaime Roveri, Michelle Sterling, Jeremiah Hahn, Brooke Walker, Sona Gevorkyan, Stefanie Cheng, Jessica Pell, Ji-In Kim, Jinsa Yoon, Hany Behkit
Photographer: Eric Laignel

Floating Stage/Viking Cruise Ship (pages 300–301, 305 [right], 320–329)
Project Team: Richard Riveire, Jennifer Mateo, Mark Borkowski, Christopher Jones, Laurence Cartledge, Eric Wattanachote, Brooke Walker, Michelle Mulitz, Gabriel Huerta, Theresa Lee, Jin Lee, Kiem Ho, Stefanie Cheng, Jennifer Porterfield, Samantha Robert, Jessica Pell, Lauren Rottet, in association with SMC Design.
Photographer: Eric Laignel

New Hotel Concept, Mexico City, Mexico (pages 330–331 [right and opposite, above]; see page 10 credits, opposite)

Luxury Residential Tower Development, New York, New York (page 331 [opposite, below])
Project Team: Lauren Rottet, David Davis, Enrique Vela, Josef Jelinek, Alana Davidson, Rose Wilkowski, Leyla Aghayeva, Kefan Lu, Ana Maria Nater
Renderers: Enrique Vela, Leyla Aghayeva, Kefan Lu

PAGE 336: See Rottet Studio, Los Angeles, California (opposite)

First published in the United States of America in 2017
by Rizzoli International Publications, Inc.
300 Park Avenue South
New York, NY 10010
www.rizzoliusa.com

Photography and project credits appear on page 334.

2017 2018 2019 2020 / 10 9 8 7 6 5 4 3 2 1

Distributed in the U.S. trade by Random House, New York

Book Design by Rita Sowins / Sowins Design

Printed in China

ISBN-13: 978-0-8478-6002-9

Library of Congress Catalog Control Number: 2017940885